HAMPTON-BROWN

HIGH POINT

SUCCESS IN LANGUAGE • LITERATURE • CONTENT

Teacher's Edition

ALFREDO SCHIFINI
DEBORAH SHORT
JOSEFINA VILLAMIL TINAJERO

HAMPTON-BROWN

Hampton-Brown
P.O. Box 223220
Carmel, California 93922
1-800-333-3510

Printed in the United States of America
0-7362-0934-4
     04 05 06 07 08 09 10 9 8 7 6 5

ACKNOWLEDGMENTS
Every effort has been made to secure permission, but if any omissions have been made, please let us know. We gratefully acknowledge permission to reprint the following material:

Susan Bergholz Literary Services: From *The House on Mango Street* by Sandra Cisneros. Copyright © 1984 by Sandra Cisneros. Published by Vintage Books, a division of Random House, Inc., and in hardcover by Alfred A. Knopf, 1994. Reprinted by permission of Susan Bergholz Literary Services, New York. All rights reserved.

Acknowledgments continue on page T422

Contents

Program Authors

Outstanding authors, experts in second-language acquisition, literacy, and content, turn research into practice for your classroom!

Dr. Alfredo Schifini assists schools across the nation and internationally in developing comprehensive ESL programs. He has worked as a high school ESL teacher, elementary reading specialist, and school administrator. Dr. Schifini directs the Southern California Professional Development Institute for teachers of ELD. Through an arrangement with Cal Poly at Pomona, he also serves as program consultant to two large teacher-training efforts in the area of reading for struggling older students. His research interests include literacy development for older second-language learners and the integration of language and content-area instruction.

CURRICULUM REVIEWERS

Tedi Armet
Fort Bend Independent School District
Sugar Land, Texas

Suzanne Barton
International Newcomer Academy
Fort Worth Independent School District
Fort Worth, Texas

Maggie Brookshire
Emerald Middle School
Cajon Valley Unified School District
El Cajon, California

Raina Cannard
Elk Grove Unified School District
El Cajon, California

Lily Dam
Dallas Independent School District
Dallas, Texas

Judy Doss
Burbank High School
Burbank Unified School District
Burbank, California

Rossana Font-Carrasco
Paul W. Bell Middle School
Miami-Dade County School District 5
Miami, Florida

Jillian Friedman
Howard Middle School
Orange County Public Schools
Orlando, Florida

Vivian Kahn
Halsey Intermediate School 296
Community School District 32
New York, New York

Suzanne Lee
Josiah Quincy School
Boston, Massachusetts

Mary McBride
Monroe Middle School
Inglewood Unified School District
Los Angeles, California

Carolyn McGavock
Rafael Cordero Bilingual Academy, Junior High School 45
Community School District 4
New York, New York

4

Dr. Deborah Short is a division director at the Center for Applied Linguistics (CAL) in Washington, D.C. She has worked as a teacher, trainer, researcher, and curriculum/materials developer. Her work at CAL has concentrated on the integration of language learning with content-area instruction. Through several national projects, she has conducted research and has provided professional development and technical assistance to local and state education agencies across the United States. She currently directs the ESL Standards and Assessment Project for TESOL.

Dr. Josefina Villamil Tinajero specializes in staff development and school–university partnership programs, and consulted with school districts in the U.S. to design ESL, bilingual, literacy, and bi-literacy programs. She has served on state and national advisory committees for standards development, including English as a New Language Advisory Panel of the National Board of Professional Teaching Standards. She is currently Professor of Education and Associate Dean at the University of Texas at El Paso, and was President of the National Association for Bilingual Education, 1997–2000.

Juan Carlos Méndez
Community School District 9
Bronx, New York

Cynthia Nelson-Mosca
Cicero School District 99
Cicero, Illinois

Kim-Anh Nguyen
Franklin McKinley School District
San Jose, California

Ellie Paiewonsky
Technical Assistance Center of Nassau
Board of Cooperative Educational Services
Massapequa Park, New York

Jeanne Perrin
Boston Public Schools
Boston, Massachusetts

Becky Peurifoy
Rockwall Independent School District
Rockwall, Texas

Marjorie Rosenberg
Montgomery County Public Schools
Rockville, Maryland

Harriet Rudnit
Grades 6–8
Lincoln Hall Middle School
Lincolnwood, Illinois

Olga Ryzhikov
Forest Oak Middle School
Montgomery County, Maryland

Dr. Wageh Saad, Ed.D.
Dearborn Public Schools
Dearborn, Michigan

Gilbert Socas
West Miami Middle School
Miami-Dade County Public Schools
Miami, Florida

HIGH POINT

Standards-Based with Specialized Instructional Strategies

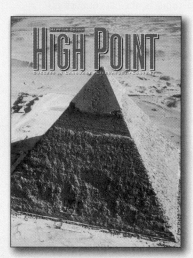

The Basics

Motivates
Struggling Readers and English Learners

➤ High interest, multicultural selections

➤ Significant themes

➤ Real-world appeal

➤ Engaging activities

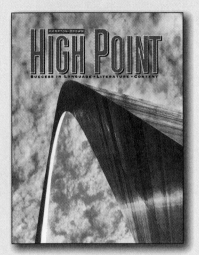

Level A

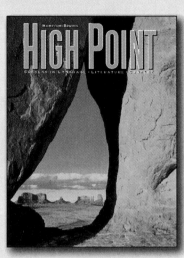

Level B

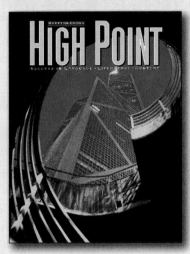

Level C

Closes Gaps in Language and Literacy

➤ Extensive vocabulary development and skills practice

➤ Complete learning to read strand

➤ Direct instruction in reading strategies

➤ Abundant use of expository text

➤ Comprehensive grammar instruction

➤ Fully supported Writing Projects

Equips Teachers for Effective Instruction

➤ Multi-level teaching strategies to address diverse needs

➤ Full array of assessment to diagnose, plan instruction, and measure progress

➤ Varied teaching tools—from transparencies to technology to tapes and theme books!

➤ Family newsletters in 7 languages to increase home involvement

Components

Integrated content across components creates a rich and contextualized learning environment. The variety of instructional tools keeps students engaged.

RESOURCES FOR STANDARDS-BASED INSTRUCTION	The Basics	LEVEL A	LEVEL B	LEVEL C
Student Books — Literature selected especially for struggling readers and English learners, instructional activities, and useful Handbooks all in one place. The Basics, Level A, Level B, Level C	●	●	●	●
The Basics Bookshelf — 18 read-aloud Theme Books for building basic vocabulary and language patterns and for developing concepts of print, listening comprehension, and knowledge of text structures	●	●	●	●
Language Tapes/CDs — Recordings of songs, poems, stories, interviews, and speeches to develop vocabulary and language		●	●	●
Selection Tapes/CDs — Readings of the Student Book selections at Levels A–C and of the Theme Books in The Basics Bookshelf	●	●	●	●
Instructional Overheads — For group instruction in grammar skills, reading strategies, and the writing process	●	●	●	●
Reading Basics — Transparencies to teach phonics and word structure plus teacher scripts, letter tiles for word building, and word tiles for high frequency word instruction.	●			

RESOURCES FOR STANDARDS-BASED INSTRUCTION	The Basics	LEVEL A	LEVEL B	LEVEL C
Practice Books — Student workbooks for skills practice The Basics · Level A · Level B · Level C	●	●	●	●
Teacher's Resource Books — Reproducible activity sheets that match the instructional overheads at Levels A–C and offer handwriting practice at The Basics, as well as family newsletters in seven languages	●	●	●	●
Diagnosis and Placement Inventory — Group-administered test for placing students into the appropriate *High Point* level based on reading and writing skills, along with a Teacher's Edition	●	●	●	●
Assessment Handbooks — A complete array of assessment tools including Language Acquisition Assessments, Selection Tests, Unit Tests, Writing Assessments, and Peer- and Self-Assessments The Basics · Level A · Level B · Level C	●	●	●	●
CD-ROM Technology — *Inspiration* Visual Learning software for making graphic organizers and mind maps	●	●	●	●
Theme Libraries — 10 books per level coordinated with unit themes and targeted to beginning, intermediate, and advanced levels		●	●	●
Teacher's Edition — Your complete resource for planning and instruction The Basics · Level A · Level B · Level C	●	●	●	●

Motivational, Real-World Content

For The Basics, 18 themes with related read-aloud Theme Books motivate students as they build a foundation in vocabulary, English structures, and early literacy skills.

LEVEL

UNIT 1	Glad to Meet You!	UNIT 7	Pack Your Bags!	UNIT
UNIT 2	Set the Table	UNIT 8	Friend to Friend	UNIT
UNIT 3	On the Job	UNIT 9	Let's Celebrate!	UNIT
UNIT 4	Numbers Count	UNIT 10	Here to Help	UNIT
UNIT 5	City Sights	UNIT 11	Make a Difference!	UNIT
UNIT 6	Welcome Home!	UNIT 12	Our Living Planet	UNIT

RESOURCES FOR STANDARDS-BASED INSTRUCTION

		The Basics	LEVEL A	LEVEL B	LEVEL C
Practice Books	Student workbooks for skills practice The Basics　Level A　Level B　Level C	●	●	●	●
Teacher's Resource Books	Reproducible activity sheets that match the instructional overheads at Levels A–C and offer handwriting practice at The Basics, as well as family newsletters in seven languages	●	●	●	●
Diagnosis and Placement Inventory	Group-administered test for placing students into the appropriate *High Point* level based on reading and writing skills, along with a Teacher's Edition	●	●	●	●
Assessment Handbooks	A complete array of assessment tools including Language Acquisition Assessments, Selection Tests, Unit Tests, Writing Assessments, and Peer- and Self-Assessments The Basics　Level A　Level B　Level C	●	●	●	●
CD-ROM Technology	*Inspiration* Visual Learning software for making graphic organizers and mind maps	●	●	●	●
Theme Libraries	10 books per level coordinated with unit themes and targeted to beginning, intermediate, and advanced levels		●	●	●
Teacher's Edition	Your complete resource for planning and instruction The Basics　Level A　Level B　Level C	●	●	●	●

Motivational, Real-World Content

For The Basics, 18 themes with related read-aloud Theme Books motivate students as they build a foundation in vocabulary, English structures, and early literacy skills.

LEVEL

UNIT 1	Glad to Meet You!	UNIT 7	Pack Your Bags!	UNIT 13	Past and Present
UNIT 2	Set the Table	UNIT 8	Friend to Friend	UNIT 14	Tell Me More
UNIT 3	On the Job	UNIT 9	Let's Celebrate!	UNIT 15	Personal Best
UNIT 4	Numbers Count	UNIT 10	Here to Help	UNIT 16	This Land is Our Land
UNIT 5	City Sights	UNIT 11	Make a Difference!	UNIT 17	Harvest Time
UNIT 6	Welcome Home!	UNIT 12	Our Living Planet	UNIT 18	Superstars

Relevant, Curriculum-Connected Themes

At Levels A–C, significant themes speak to issues of interest for students, connect to middle school content, and offer instructional choices for teachers.

LEVEL **A**

LEVEL **B**

LEVEL **C**

	Identity	Communication	Personal Expression
UNIT 1	Identity	Communication	Personal Expression
UNIT 2	Cooperation	Belonging	Discoveries
UNIT 3	Relationships	Dreams and Decisions	Conflict and Resolution
UNIT 4	Community	Continuity and Change	Choices
UNIT 5	Traditions	Challenges	Triumphs

Standards-Based Instruction for All Students

*Curriculum Standards provide the foundation for **High Point**. Carefully selected readings and specially designed lessons with Multi-Level Strategies ensure standards-based instruction for struggling readers and English learners!*

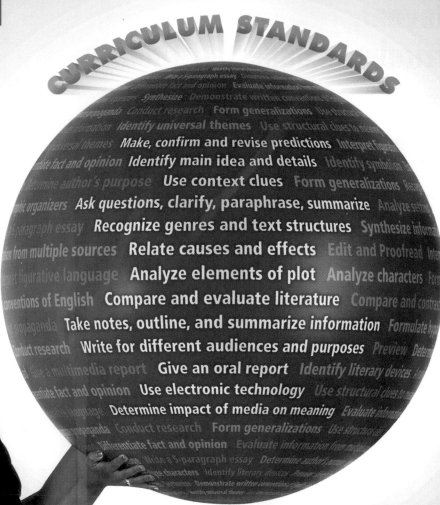

CURRICULUM STANDARDS

Make, confirm and revise predictions
Identify main idea and details
Use context clues
Ask questions, clarify, paraphrase, summarize
Recognize genres and text structures
Relate causes and effects
Analyze elements of plot
Analyze characters
Compare and evaluate literature
Take notes, outline, and summarize information
Write for different audiences and purposes
Give an oral report
Use electronic technology
Determine impact of media on meaning

DIFFERENTIATED INSTRUCTION FOR EACH STANDARD

Multi-Level Strategies
ACTIVITY OPTIONS FOR ANALYZING ELEMENTS OF PLOT

BEGINNING Read the myth aloud, pausing after each event to clarify meaning. Have students sketch the event. Select and save one sketch per event. After reading, draw a rising-and-falling action map. Review the myth as you place the sketches on the map. Create a group sentence about each step in the plot: *A conflict happens when Hades steals Demeter's daughter.*

INTERMEDIATE Read the myth aloud or play its recording. Pause after key events to elicit steps in the plot: *What is the conflict about?* Work as a group to record events on the rising-and-falling action map on **Transparency 72**. After reading, partners retell the myth to each other.

ADVANCED As partners read the myth or listen to its recording, have them complete the plot diagram on **Master 72**. After reading, students retell the myth to each other. Then have students change an event and revise the plot diagram before telling the story again to see how events in the plot affect the final outcome.

Complete Skills Coverage

The **High Point** Scope and Sequence covers the full range of skills English learners need for academic success.

SCOPE AND SEQUENCE	The Basics	LEVEL A	LEVEL B	LEVEL C
Language Development and Communication	•	•	•	•
Language Functions	•	•	•	•
Language Patterns and Structures	•	•	•	•
Concepts and Vocabulary	•	•	•	•
Reading	•	•	•	•
Learning to Read: concepts of print, phonemic awareness, phonics, decoding, and word recognition	•			
Reading Strategies	•	•	•	•
Comprehension	•	•	•	•
Literary Analysis and Appreciation		•	•	•
Speaking, Listening, Viewing, Representing	•	•	•	•
Cognitive Academic Skills	•	•	•	•
Learning Strategies	•	•	•	•
Critical Thinking	•	•	•	•
Research Skills	•	•	•	•
Writing	•	•	•	•
Handwriting	•			
Writing Modes and Forms	•		•	•
Writing Process			•	•
Writer's Craft		•	•	•
Grammar, Usage, Mechanics, Spelling	•	•	•	•
Technology / Media		•	•	•
Cultural Perspectives	•	•	•	•

Assessment To Inform Instruction

High Point includes a comprehensive array of assessment tools to place students at the appropriate level, to monitor students' progress, and to assess mastery of the Language Arts standards.

DIAGNOSIS AND PLACEMENT

Diagnosis and Placement Inventory

This group-administered test places students into the appropriate *High Point* level based on reading and writing skills. A Teacher's Edition contains additional diagnostic tools, including reading fluency assessments, and provides guidance on administering the test, scoring, and interpreting results.

PROGRESS MONITORING AND SUMMATIVE EVALUATION

These assessments appear in the Assessment Handbook for each level.

Language Acquisition Assessment

Identifies Performance Assessment opportunities in each unit and offers scoring rubrics to monitor the student's progress through the stages of language proficiency.

Selection Tests

At Levels A–C, multiple-choice items and short-answer questions measure mastery of the reading strategies and the vocabulary, comprehension, and language arts skills taught with each reading selection.

Unit Tests in Standardized Test Format

The multiple-choice sections of these tests for all levels measure students' cumulative understanding of skills and language. Writing Prompts for all levels measure progress in writing skills and fluency. At Levels A–C, the Read, Think, and Explain sections offer open-ended items to measure strategies and comprehension.

Writing Assessment

A Writing Progress Checklist is used to evaluate writing in The Basics. At Levels A–C, scoring rubrics offer guidance in evaluating students' work for the Writing Project in each unit. These rubrics assist teachers in assessing how students might score on a similar task if it were encountered on a standardized test by looking at content, form, and written conventions.

Self-Assessment and Peer-Assessment Forms

Students use these forms to evaluate their work and offer feedback to their classmates.

Portfolio Evaluation Form

Students and teachers use this form to evaluate progress shown by the work collected in the portfolio.

Diagnosis and Placement Inventory

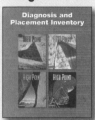

Student Test   Teacher's Edition

Assessment Handbooks

The Basics   Level A

Level B   Level C

PROGRAM GUIDE FOR
Assessment and Instruction

PROGRAM GUIDE FOR
Assessment and Instruction

HIGH POINT

Program Guide for Assessment and Instruction

Program Goals and Organization

High Point offers standards-based instruction in reading and language arts. The program is carefully designed for English learners and struggling readers to accelerate their growth in language and literacy.

Four overlapping levels proceed on a continuum from The Basics, a beginning language and literacy level, to Level C, the most advanced level. From Level C, students move to study in mainstream materials.

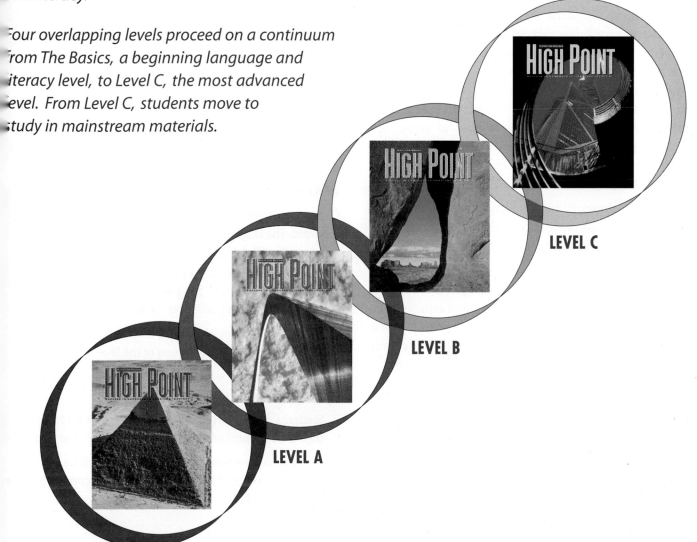

LEVEL C

LEVEL B

LEVEL A

THE BASICS

Identifying Students Who Need *High Point*

INITIAL IDENTIFICATION

High Point addresses the needs of struggling readers and English learners. To identify students who should study in *High Point*, consider information from assessments, such as the following:

- Standardized tests measure student performance in relation to a national norm. These tests report a student's percentile rank. Students scoring below the percentile rank set by your district, generally the 25th percentile, need the intervention program.

- Other tests report a student's reading level. Students whose reading level is two or more years below their grade level need the intervention program.

- A reading fluency measure, such as Edformation's *Standard Benchmark Reading Fluency Assessment Passages* available through Hampton-Brown, can also be used to determine reading level. Start by giving the student the fluency measure for the grade two years lower than the student's actual grade. If the number of words read correctly per minute by the student is lower than the mean for that grade level, the student should receive the intervention program.

- For English learners, districts are required to give a test that measures language proficiency level. Use the information from this test to identify students who need English language development.

The students identified for instruction in *High Point* come from a variety of backgrounds and educational experiences. Some have not yet learned to decode or have basic decoding skills but have not yet learned to apply them to multisyllabic words. Others possess decoding skills, but need to learn about text structures and the strategies of reading so that they can access grade-level materials and be successful in academic tasks.

Some English learners bring a solid educational foundation from their native country. In their home language they have developed academic skills that are on a par with their native English-speaking counterparts. Even if these students are literate in a language with a non-Roman alphabet and have the challenge of a new written code to crack, they already bring many of the skills and experiences they need to succeed in a structured academic setting.

Other English learners come from a patchwork of academic and life experiences. War, epidemics, natural disasters, or economic conditions may have caused students and their families to relocate within their home country or in other countries even before arriving in the U.S. School attendance may have been sporadic, with acquisition of skills and content more random than systematic. Limited academic experiences and the lack of formal literacy skills create special challenges for these students and their teachers.

High Point will help you meet these challenges. The Basics level teaches students how to decode and comprehend text up to a third-grade level. The direct, spiraling instruction in text structures, reading strategies and comprehension skills in Levels A–C builds reading power, moving students to a sixth grade reading level. Coupled with the reading instruction is a complete language development strand to support English learners as well as struggling readers who may also need to broaden their vocabularies and to gain facility with the structures of English.

> **Correct placement is crucial to students' success in the program.**

DIAGNOSIS AND PLACEMENT

Correct placement is crucial to students' success in the program. The *Diagnosis and Placement Inventory* that accompanies *High Point* provides for six placement points into the materials. Students who need decoding skills will begin in The Basics level. See page 17 for the scope and sequence of decoding skills and the three placement points:

1. Non-readers and newly-arrived English learners will be placed at the beginning of the level.

2. Students with some literacy skills will be placed before the work on long vowels begins in Unit 5.

3. Students who can decode but still need to learn to apply their skills to multisyllabic words will be placed at Unit 14.

Students who have mastered decoding skills will be placed at the beginning of Level A, Level B, or Level C according to their reading level and the array of skills mastered on the *Diagnosis and Placement Inventory*.

Placement Points in *High Point*

The *Diagnosis and Placement Inventory* surveys students' reading and writing skills to present a student profile of strengths and weaknesses and place students into ***High Point***. Students who are reading severely below grade level are likely to place in The Basics level because they need the phonics and decoding skills shown below. These are listed for the purpose of clarifying the placement points. The Basics level, like Levels A–C, contains a balance of skills in vocabulary development, reading comprehension, writing strategies and applications, and written and oral English conventions. The Student Profile that is generated from the administration of the *Diagnosis and Placement Inventory* presents a picture of where students stand in all these skills areas.

		THE BASICS Reading/Lexile Levels: Grades 1-3
Placement Point 1 →	LAKESIDE SCHOOL	Letters and Sounds
	UNIT 1	Short Vowels
	UNIT 2	Short Vowels and Digraphs
	UNIT 3	Short Vowels, Digraphs, and Double Consonants
	UNIT 4	Blends and Digraphs
Placement Point 2 →	UNIT 5	Long Vowels, Word Patterns, and Multisyllabic Words
	UNIT 6	Long Vowels and Word Patterns
	UNIT 7	Long Vowels and Word Patterns
	UNIT 8	Inflections
	UNIT 9	Inflections
	UNIT 10	Long Vowels
	UNIT 11	*R*-controlled Vowels
	UNIT 12	Multisyllabic Words
	UNIT 13	Words with *y*
Placement Point 3 →	UNIT 14	Diphthongs and Variant Vowels
	UNIT 15	Variant Vowels and Consonants
	UNIT 16	Multisyllabic Words
	UNIT 17	Multisyllabic Words (Suffixes and Prefixes)
	UNIT 18	Multisyllabic Words
Placement Point 4 →		LEVEL A Reading/Lexile Level: Grade 4
Placement Point 5 →		LEVEL B Reading/Lexile Level: Grade 5
Placement Point 6 →		LEVEL C Reading/Lexile Level: Grade 6

Assessment to Inform Instruction

ASSESSMENT TOOLS

High Point offers a comprehensive array of assessment tools to inform instruction. These tools will help you place students into the program, monitor their progress, and evaluate their achievement both in language acquisition and in the language arts standards. These tools and the spiraling curriculum work together to ensure that students receive the instruction they need to accelerate their growth in language and literacy.

Assessment Tool	Description	Entry Level and Placement	Progress Monitoring	Summative Evaluation
Standard Benchmark Reading Fluency Assessment Passages	Three graded and equivalent passages are provided for each grade and are designed for administration at the beginning, middle, and end of the year. Administration of the passages identifies the student's fluency rate measured in words read correctly per minute (wcpm). This fluency rate can be compared to normative performance in order to identify students who need instruction in **High Point** or to assess their progress and achievement. Passages are available for license and downloading at www.edformation.com/hampton-brown .	✔	✔	✔
Diagnosis and Placement Inventory	This inventory surveys the skills taught in each level. It provides for six placement points into the program and gives a picture of the student's strengths and weaknesses in specific skills areas.	✔		
Language Acquisition Assessments	These assessments identify opportunities in each unit for performance assessments in which you can evaluate how well students demonstrate the language functions and structures targeted in the unit.		✔	
Decoding Progress Checks	At The Basics level, these word lists can be used on a weekly basis to monitor attainment of the targeted phonics skills.		✔	
Selection Tests	At Levels A–C, twenty tests, one per main selection, measure students' progress in reading strategies and vocabulary, comprehension, and language arts skills taught with the main selection.		✔	

Assessment Tool	Description	Entry Level and Placement	Progress Monitoring	Summative Evaluation
Standard Progress Monitoring Reading Fluency Assessment Passages	Weekly graded and equivalent passages are provided for each grade. By measuring the number of words read correctly on the passages across several weeks, you can monitor a student's progress and plan effective instruction. Passages are available for license and downloading at www.edformation.com/hampton-brown .		✔	
Writing Assessments	At Levels A–C, these assessments, one per unit, provide rubrics and scoring guidelines for evaluating a student's writing in the mode and form targeted in each unit's writing project.		✔	
Writing Checklist / Writing Progress and Conference Form	These forms can be used to evaluate any writing done by the students and to hold writing conferences.		✔	
Self-Assessment Forms	These forms enable students to evaluate their own work.		✔	
Peer-Assessment Form	This form provides a vehicle for peer feedback on a variety of student work.		✔	
Portfolio Evaluation Form	This form serves as a record of both teacher- and student-selected samples in the portfolio and provides for summarizing performance.		✔	
Unit Tests	These tests, one for every three units at The Basics level and one for every unit at Levels A, B, or C, measure students' achievement.			✔
Student-Profile: Year-End	This form organizes information obtained from both formal and informal assessment and provides a permanent record of performance.			✔

Reading Instruction in *High Point*

Learning to Read in The Basics

In each unit, students learn high frequency words, phonics skills, and decoding strategies, then apply them in decodable text.

❶ The Basics introduces 266 high frequency words. Students see them, hear them, say them, spell them, and use them in word work activities to help commit them to memory. They then read the words in context to develop automatic recognition.

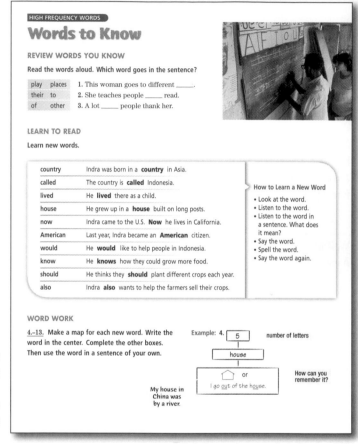

High Frequency Word Instruction from Unit 11 of The Basics Student Book

Practice

*The **Reading Practice Book** and additional reinforcement activities in the Teacher's Edition provide sufficient repetitions to build skills mastery.*

High Frequency Word Practice in the Reading Practice Book

❷ Transparencies help you build the meaning of words used in decoding activities, introduce phonics skills, model decoding strategies, and direct the guided practice. **Teacher Scripts** are in the Teacher's Edition and in a separate booklet to facilitate instruction at the overhead.

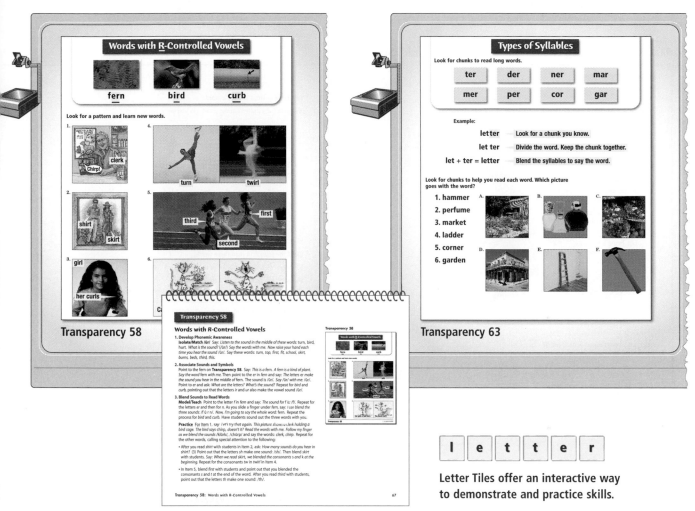

Transparency 58

Transparency 63

Teacher Scripts

Letter Tiles offer an interactive way to demonstrate and practice skills.

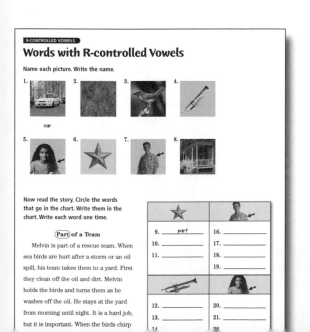

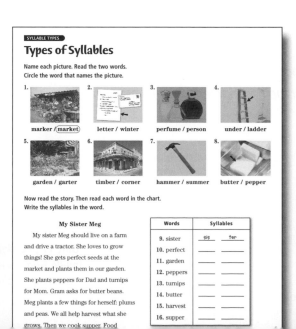

Phonics Practice and Decodable Text in the Reading Practice Book

Learning to Read in The Basics, continued

❸ Next, in the Student Book, students review the skills, try the decoding strategy on their own, read decodable text, spell words with the new phonetic element, and participate in hands-on activities that anchor their understanding of the new skill.

Reading and Spelling Pages from Unit 11 of The Basics Student Book

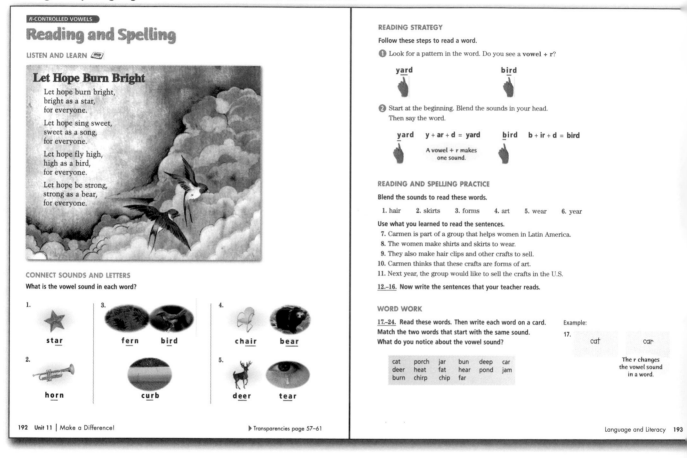

Practice

*The **Reading Practice Book** offers plenty of opportunities to read decodable text and build reading fluency.*

**Unit 11 Decodable Book
(made from pages of the
Reading Practice Book)**

4 Students then apply phonics skills and read the pretaught high frequency words as they read and respond to a decodable selection.

Read on Your Own Pages from Unit 11 of The Basics Student Book

COMPREHENSION: CLASSIFY INFORMATION

Read on Your Own

Nadja Halilbegovich is from Bosnia.

Hafsat Abiola is from Nigeria.

Craig Kielburger is from Canada.

Kids Are Helping Kids

Kids can help other kids in important ways. Nadja, Hafsat, and Craig show us how.

Nadja helped kids in Bosnia. When Nadja was a girl, ethnic groups in Bosnia started a war. Kids lived in fear. A lot of them were hurt. Nadja started a radio show. She sang on the air to give children courage. She also published two books. They tell how hard it is to live through a war. She hopes her books will help end fighting in the world.

Hafsat helps kids in Nigeria. She formed a group called KIND. The group teaches children their rights. It shows kids how to be leaders. KIND also helps women and children get fair treatment.

Craig was 12 years old when he read that many kids were made to work in hard jobs for no pay. People treated them very badly. He had to help these kids. He formed a group called Free the Children. Now, his group speaks out for children's rights in 27 countries.

194   Unit 11 | Make a Difference!

CHECK YOUR UNDERSTANDING

1.–3. Copy the chart and then complete it.

Who Helped Others?	Where?	What Group of People Did He or She Help?	How?
1. Nadja Halilbegovich	Bosnia	children	She published two books. She started a radio show.

EXPAND YOUR VOCABULARY

4.–6. Tell a partner about each person on page 194. Use information from your chart and some of these words and phrases.

brings hope	fair treatment	hard jobs
sang on the air	rights	formed a group
war	published	Free the Children

Example: 4. Nadja published two books.
             The books tell about the war in Bosnia.

WRITE ABOUT PEOPLE ✏

7. Choose one of the kids from page 194 or another person you know. Tell how the person makes a difference.

Example: 7. Craig helps kids who were made to work in hard jobs.
             He formed a group called Free the Children.

Language and Literacy   195

COMPREHENSION

Build Reading Fluency

Read the article. Stop when the timer goes off. Mark your score.
Then try it again two more times on different days.

Another Kid Helps Kids

Kimmie Weeks started making a difference when he was 10. The year was 1991. His country, Liberia, was at war. Many homes and schools were destroyed. Hundreds of children had no food. Many were sick. The fighting was so bad, children were trained to be soldiers. No one seemed to know what to do. Kimmie felt he had to help.

He and other kids started cleaning the streets. They picked up bricks, stones, and other trash left after the fighting. Then he started speaking on the radio. He said that children should not fight in war. His speeches helped. In 1996, Liberia stopped training children to fight.

Kimmie is now a young man. He is still helping the children of his country. He raises money to open more schools. Today, many children have better lives thanks to Kimmie Weeks.

Timed Passage for Reading Fluency from Unit 11 of the Reading Practice Book

	Day 1	Day 2	Day 3
Total Words Read in One Minute			
Minus Words Missed			

Building Reading Power in Levels A–C

Once students have learned to decode in The Basics, they build reading power through the increasingly more difficult selections in Levels A–C.

Within and across levels:

- Reading level advances
- Length of selections increases
- Text density builds
- Picture/text correspondence decreases
- Vocabulary and concept loads progress
- Sentence structure and verb tenses increase in complexity

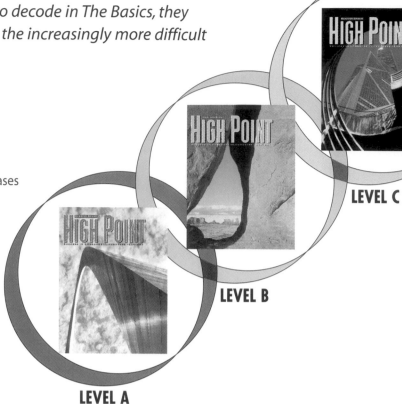

LEVEL C

LEVEL B

LEVEL A

Level A

THE WORLD TODAY

Today, our common resources are being used up.

*T*oday the world is much like that village. Now our commons are our parks, **reserves**, and **natural resources**, and the waters and air of the whole world. Today we have almost the same problem that the villagers had.

Today each fisherman tries to catch as many fish as he can from the common sea. This way, the fisherman has more fish to sell—**in the short run**. But soon there are fewer and fewer fish. This is not good for the fish, the sea, or for the people.

Today each **lumber company** wants to cut down as many trees as it can, to sell for wood, paper, and **fuel**. The more trees the lumber company cuts down, the more money it makes—in the short run. But after cutting down so many trees, there are fewer and fewer **forests**. This is not good for the trees, or for the **forest creatures**, or the forest **soil**.

BEFORE YOU MOVE ON...

1. **Vocabulary** *In the short run* means "now." What do you think *in the long run* means?
2. **Details** The villagers almost used up all the grass on the commons. List two resources that we are in danger of using up today.
3. **Cause and Effect** What would happen if we used all the fish and trees now?

---
reserves land that is saved for a special reason
in the short run now, at the present time
lumber company company that cuts down trees for use in making products
fuel something used to give heat and power
forest creatures animals that live in the woods
soil dirt, ground, earth

Today each fisherman tries to catch as many fish as he can.

This is not good for the fish, the sea or for the people.

Today each lumber company wants to cut down as many trees as it can. This is not good for the trees, or the forest creatures, or the forest soil.

Level B

THE SILENT YEARS

The twins' parents discover that Suzy and Neshy are deaf. They all learn sign language so everyone in the family can communicate with each other.

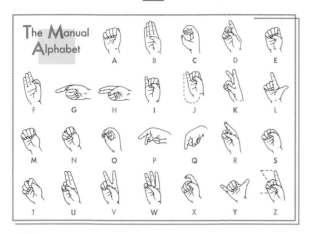

The Manual Alphabet

A B C D E
F G H I J K L
M N O P Q R S
T U V W X Y Z

Early on they knew they were different from other children, because they were the only ones who shared a face. "They loved that about themselves," says Maria Aguayo, mother of Neshmayda and Suzette. "They had a way of communicating that no one else understood. One of them would point at something or make some noise and the other would go and get what she wanted." Two kids **cavorting through** a happy world of their own, experiencing life's surprises as one—in other words, twins.

But Suzy and Neshy were different for a much greater reason—they were born **deaf**.

---

cavorting through having fun in

deaf without the ability to hear

160 Unit 3 | Dreams and Decisions

"We did not know it for their first two-and-a-half years," says Maria, who **contracted** German measles during her first **trimester**. The technology in her native Puerto Rico was not as **advanced** as it is today, so her twins' deafness was not **diagnosed** until they were nearly three. "And when we first discovered they were deaf, I did not want to believe it. It was a mother's denial."

Maria soon accepted her daughters' **condition**, and as soon as she and her husband, Joaquin, heard about the Gallaudet school for the deaf in Washington, D.C., they moved their family and enrolled the twins,

Suzette (left) and Neshmayda (right) at age six. The twins are wearing hearing aids strapped to their chests as they enjoy a day at Baltimore's Inner Harbor.

then five years old. "We all learned **sign language** so we could communicate with the girls," says Maria. "We started to talk about all the things that had happened to them in their first five years. I learned all these things that I had not known. For instance, Suzette had once been with her grandmother and **wound up** in the emergency room **getting stitches**. Her grandmother didn't know how she got hurt. Suzy later told me that she had fallen, that she was scared, that she wanted me there with her in the hospital **so badly**. When I discovered these things, I cried and cried."

> **BEFORE YOU MOVE ON...**
> 1. **Inference** What do you think helped the twins form their own way of communicating?
> 2. **Cause and Effect** What caused the twins' deafness, and why did it take so long to diagnose?
> 3. **Prediction** Do you think the twins will remain close as they grow up? Why or why not?

---

contracted got, caught
trimester three months of being pregnant
diagnosed discovered by doctors
sign language a way to communicate with our hands

wound up in the end was
getting stitches having her cut or wound closed by sewing
so badly so much

Twins 161

Level C

CINQUÉ PLEADS FOR FREEDOM

Instead of Africa, the *Amistad* arrives in America. The Africans remain prisoners until Cinqué and his ally, John Adams, win their freedom in court.

But they had **claimed victory** too soon. Cinqué ordered the Spaniards to steer the ship toward the rising sun. They obeyed and sailed the ship east toward Africa during the day, but then at night turned the ship around and sailed northwest toward North America.

For two months the ship **pitched** back and forth across the Atlantic Ocean. Eight more Africans died during that time—some from their battle wounds, some from food poisoning, and some from starvation.

Then on August 27, 1839, the *Amistad* was **escorted** by an American ship into the harbor of New London, Connecticut. Weary, hungry, and hopelessly lost, Cinqué and the others were forced to come ashore.

An American naval lieutenant saw the possibility for quick **profits** in the Africans. But this was the North, and a group of whites and free blacks **campaigning against** the **institution of slavery** was gaining popularity. They called themselves **abolitionists**, and they took on Cinqué and the other Africans as their most important **case**.

The Africans were sent to prison in New Haven, Connecticut, until a decision could be made.

The abolitionists managed to find a translator, and Cinqué told his story in a U.S. court. He was only twenty-five years old, but his experience on the *Amistad* had given him the confidence of a much older man.

The courtroom was crowded, and many were moved by Cinqué's **impassioned words**.

"I am not here to argue the case against slavery," Cinqué said, "though I will say it is a sin against man and God. I am here to argue the facts. The **indisputable**, international law is that the stealing of slaves from Africa is now **illegal**."

"The men who kidnapped us, who beat and tortured us, were—and are—guilty of this crime," Cinqué continued.

"We are a peaceful people. We regret the loss of life caused by our **mutiny**. But we are not savages. We took over the ship to save our lives. We have done no wrong. Allow us to go home."

The weekend before the judge made his decision, Cinqué and his companions waited in the New Haven jail, their hearts filled with fear and hope. The judge held the power to make the Africans slaves or to set them free. On Monday morning, January 13, 1840, they worried no longer. He had decided they should be returned home.

They were free.

"We have done no wrong."

But as Cinqué was soon to learn, the passage to freedom was as winding as the *Amistad*'s journey across the sea. President Martin Van Buren, concerned that freeing the Mende would enrage southern slave holders, ordered the district attorney to **file an appeal** so the case would be heard in the U.S. Supreme Court. And because of this, Cinqué gained his greatest American **ally**: former president John Quincy Adams.

Having heard about the mutineers, Adams came out of **retirement** to argue Cinqué's case. He was seventy-two years old. It had been more than thirty years since he had argued a case in a courtroom, and the thought of bearing the responsibility for this one worried the elderly statesman deeply.

But inspired by Cinqué, whom many of the abolitionists had begun to refer to as the Black Prince, Adams tirelessly prepared his **defense**. In court he spoke on behalf of the Mende for eight and a half hours. Sweat poured from his brow, and his voice filled the packed courtroom as he presented his case.

---

claimed victory thought they won
pitched rocked
escorted guided, led, accompanied

profits earned money, income
campaigning against trying to convince others to stop
institution of slavery tradition of keeping slaves

impassioned words speech full of emotion
indisputable not-to-be-questioned
mutiny fight to take over the ship

file an appeal request a new trial
ally friend, supporter
retirement the private life he had since he quit working

170 Unit 3 Conflict and Resolution

Amistad Rising 171

Explicit Skills Instruction

Instructional Overheads allow the teacher to present instruction explicitly.

TEXT FEATURES

This Overhead explains how to read for information. The Teacher's Edition tells the teacher how to model the skill and conduct guided practice. Students then apply the skill immediately as they read the article in the Student Book.

HOW TO READ FOR INFORMATION

Directions: Use these strategies when you look at photos, maps, and diagrams.

Much of San Francisco was in ruins after the 1906 earthquake.

Photos and Captions

1. Look at the photo. Ask yourself: What does it show?
2. Read the caption. Think about how it explains the photo.

Maps

1. Use the compass rose to see which direction is north, south, east, and west on the map.
2. Use the legend to find out what symbols on the map mean.
3. Use the scale of miles to estimate distance.
4. Read titles or captions, to help you understand what the map shows.

California's San Andreas Fault

Diagrams

1. Look at the picture.
2. Read the labels, captions, and other text.
3. Describe what you see. Explain what the picture shows in your own words.

When plates move against each other, pressure is created.

Transparency 68   Level A, Unit 4 | Community   © Hampton-

Level A Instructional Overhead

Level A Student Book

Hurricane in the Caribbean, 1998

MONDAY, SEPTEMBER 21, 1998

Hurricane Georges Hits Puerto Rico

Hurricane Georges slammed into the island of Puerto Rico at around 6 p.m. today. Winds **reached** over 115 miles per hour. Airplanes flipped over like toys. Trees were **uprooted** and flew through the air like missiles. Over 80 percent of the island is without electricity. Seventy percent of all homes are without water.

Inside a Hurricane

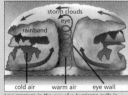

Low pressure in the eye of a hurricane pulls in cooler air, creating a powerful storm with winds over 74 miles per hour.

The path of Hurricane Georges

TUESDAY, SEPTEMBER 22, 1998

Georges Blasts Dominican Republic— Rescue Efforts Begin

Hurricane Georges spreads its destruction to the Dominican Republic. **Mudslides** and **flooding** kill over 200 people. More than 100,000 people are left **homeless**.

Meanwhile, rescue workers bring aid to Puerto Rico. More than 20,000 people **crowd into shelters** in San Juan and other cities.

FRIDAY, SEPTEMBER 25, 1998

Hurricane Relief Underway

Rescue workers in the Dominican Republic and Haiti **struggle** to bring food, water, and shelter to people. House

after house **lies in ruins** or without a roof.

"There's no water. There's no power. There is nothing," says Domingo Osvaldo Fortuna as he fills a plastic jug with water from the garbage-filled Ozama River in Santo Domingo.

Aid from the United States begins to arrive. A French cargo plane brings **relief workers**, food, and medicine. Sixty-three firefighters from New York help to search for survivors.

SUNDAY, SEPTEMBER 27, 1998

Hurricane Continues— Tons of Food On the Way

Tons of food and supplies begin to arrive in the Dominican Republic and Haiti. Volunteers fly in with tons of bottled water and enough **plastic sheeting** to repair 15,000 houses. Members of the U.S. military carry aid to towns **cut off by** flooding and mudslides.

Although it will take weeks or even years for the islands to **repair** the **damage**, **recovery** has slowly begun.

POINT-BY-POINT

HOW COMMUNITIES RESPOND TO DISASTERS

After a Hurricane:

- Emergency shelters are set up for people who are left homeless.
- Rescue workers bring food, water, and medicine to disaster victims.
- Rescue workers search for survivors.
- The international community sends aid to help victims recover and rebuild.

BEFORE YOU MOVE ON...

1. **Vocabulary** What words or phrases describe the strength of the hurricane?
2. **Cause and Effect** What problems did the hurricane cause?
3. **Details** How did other countries help the people on the islands?

---

reached got as fast as
uprooted pulled from the ground
Mudslides Rushing rivers of mud and rain

flooding water overflowing the banks of rivers
homeless without homes, with nowhere to live
crowd into are pushed together in

lies in ruins sits on the ground in pieces
Tons Several thousands of pounds
plastic sheeting waterproof covering

cut off by unable to have contact with the outside world because of
repair fix, correct

246   Unit 4 | Community

When Disaster Strikes   **247**

TEXT STRUCTURES

This Overhead outlines the structures of different kinds of text and the corresponding reading strategies. The Teacher's Edition tells the teacher how to model the strategies and conduct guided practice. Students immediately apply the strategies to paired selections about ancient China, one fictional and one informational.

RECOGNIZE FICTION AND NONFICTION

Name _____ Date _____

Directions: Preview the text. Then, use the diagram to help you decide if the text is fiction or nonfiction. Follow the suggestions at the bottom as you read.

Step 1

Think about author's purpose for writing.
- to tell a story
- to entertain
- to give you information

Step 2

Think about your purpose for reading.
- for enjoyment
- for information

Step 3

Decide if the text is fiction or nonfiction.

For fiction, do the following:
- Identify characters and settings.
- Identify the sequence of events in the plot.
- Identify new words.

For nonfiction, do the following:
- Slow down your reading.
- Identify facts about real people or events.
- Pay attention to new words.
- Concentrate as you read.

Master 80 Unit 5 | Traditions   83

Level A Instructional Overhead

Level A Student Book: Fiction and Nonfiction

HOW THE Ox Star FELL FROM Heaven

by Lily Toy Hong

This ancient Chinese story tells about a message that gets mixed up. It also explains why people use oxen to help grow crops for food.

LI...

Long ago, the...

In the beginning, ... on Earth. They could o... **the heavens**, among th... with the Emperor of Al... his Imperial Palace.

Clothed in robes of the finest **silk**, they **reclined** on **billowy** clouds. They never had to work, and their lives were easy.

Life on Earth was hard, especially hard since oxen did not live here. Farmers had no **beast of burden** to help with the planting of vegetables and rice in the spring, or with the gathering of **crops** at **harvest time**.

People were always tired and hungry. They **labored** from **sunup** to **sundown**, yet they could never finish all their work.

Because there was so little food, they sometimes went three, four, even five days without **one single meal**.

the heavens the sky
silk soft, shiny cloth
reclined leaned back, rested
billowy soft and fluffy
beast of burden animal used for heavy work
one single meal one meal to eat, anything to eat

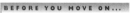

BEFORE YOU MOVE ON...

1. **Details** What made life on Earth difficult for the farmers?
2. **Comparisons** How were the lives of the oxen and the humans different?
3. **Prediction** This story describes what life was like "in the beginning." How do you think the story may change by the end?

Ancient China during the Zhou Dynasty, 1050 BCE–256 CE

A Peasant's Life in ANCIENT CHINA

an article by Shirleyann Costigan

Life was never easy for the peasant farmers of ancient China. They worked the earth, planted, and **harvested** the crops by hand. It was slow, **backbreaking** work. Around 700 BCE, many farmers began to use oxen or water buffalo to pull the plows and seed the fields. **Food production increased**. Everyone ate better. Life got a little easier, but not by much.

Most peasants lived in small villages near the **manor houses** of their **lords**. Their small huts were made of **packed earth** with dirt floors. Peasants rented the land they lived and worked on. They gave a large part of every

In ancient China, the lords and scholars lived in big houses and dressed in silks. They

CLASSES OF SOCIETY IN ANCIENT CHINA, 700 BCE

There were three classes of people under the Emperor of ancient China. The people of each class had a place to fill in the Chinese order of life. The order rarely changed.

Emperor the Son of Heaven

Lords & Scholars rulers of the land

Knights protectors of the land

Peasant farmers worked from sunup to sundown all year long. They also had to work on roads and canals that ran through the countryside.

Rice

Peasants grew their own food, as well as food for the ruling classes. Rice, soybeans, and millet were all common crops.

Soybeans

Millet

Spiraling Instruction

*Instruction in **High Point** spirals across the levels and is tailored to students' increasing literacy and language skills.*

Level A Instructional Overhead

Level A

This level introduces self-monitoring strategies. Teachers use the Instructional Overhead to model the strategy and conduct guided practice. Students then use a simple Note-Taking Chart to apply the strategy as they read.

A DOG YOU CAN COUNT ON

from *A Guide Dog Puppy Grows Up*
by Caroline Arnold

It takes a lot of training to be a guide dog for the blind. That's because guide dog owners really count on their furry friends. This article shows how they learn to work together.

Stacy will teach Moe how to work with his new guide dog.

When Moe Enguillado **arrives** to begin his **guide dog** training, Stacy Burrow **greets** him. She is one of his **instructors**. Moe is excited about getting a dog. At the same time, he is a little **worried** about everything he will have to learn.

Stacy knows the dogs very well. Each dog has its own **personality**. After meeting the new students, Stacy carefully **matches each person with** one of the dogs.

Level A Student Book

Name _____ Date _____

NOTE-TAKING CHART

Directions: After you read each paragraph, stop to ask questions. Write your questions. Reread to find information. Write your answers or your best guess.

A Dog You Can Count On

Page	Your Questions	Your Answers
Page 96		
Page 97		
Page 98		

**Level A
Note-Taking Chart**

Levels B and C

These levels show the spiraling instruction. The Instructional Overhead introduces new aspects of the self-monitoring strategy—summarizing and predicting. Students use more advanced Note-Taking Charts as they read.

HOW TO MONITOR YOUR READING

Directions: Read the passage. Then read and answer the questions in the chart below. Try to think of other questions that would help you understand the reading better.

Wednesday, July 8, 1942

Dearest Kitty,

It seems like years since Sunday morning. So much has happened. It's as if the whole world had suddenly turned upside down. But as you can see, Kitty, I'm still alive, and that's the main thing, Father says. I'm alive all right, but don't ask where or how. You probably don't understand a word I'm saying, so I'll begin by telling you what happened Sunday afternoon.

Clarify	**Ask Questions**
What words need more explanation?	What questions did I have while I was reading?
Summarize	**Predict**
What does the author want us to remember from this reading?	What will the next section of the reading be about?

Transparency 66 Level B, Unit 4 | Continuity and Change   © Hampton-Brown

Level B Instructional Overhead

---

from The
Diary
of a
Young
Girl

BY ANNE FRANK

---

he will be taken away to a concentration camp.

WEDNESDAY, JULY 8, 1942

Dearest Kitty,

It seems like years since Sunday morning. So much has happened it's as if the whole world had suddenly turned upside down. But as you can see, Kitty, I'm still alive, and that's the **main thing**, Father says. I'm alive all right, but don't ask where or how. You probably don't understand a word I'm saying, so I'll begin by telling you what happened Sunday afternoon.

At three o'clock (Hello* had left but was supposed to come back later), the doorbell rang. I didn't hear it, since I was out on the balcony, lazily reading in the sun. A little while later Margot appeared in the kitchen doorway looking very **agitated**. "Father has received a **call-up notice** from **the SS**," she whispered. "Mother has gone to see Mr. van Daan." (Mr. van Daan is Father's **business partner** and a good friend.)

I was **stunned**. A call-up: everyone knows what that means. **Visions** of concentration camps and lonely **cells** raced through my head. How could we let Father go to such a fate? "Of course he's not going," declared Margot as we waited for Mother in the living room. "Mother's gone to Mr. van Daan to ask whether we can move to our hiding place tomorrow. The van Daans are going with us. There will be seven of us altogether." Silence. We couldn't speak. The thought of Father off visiting someone in the Jewish Hospital and completely **unaware of** what was happening, the long wait for Mother, the heat, the **suspense**—all this **reduced us to silence**.

cells rooms in a prison
unaware of not knowing
suspense fear, tension
reduced us to silence made us unable to speak

Level B Student Book

Name _____ Date _____

HOW TO MONITOR YOUR READING

Directions: Use the four strategies on this chart to monitor your reading. Fill in the boxes as you read each section of the selection.

Clarify	**Ask Questions**
• One of the words I wasn't sure about was _____ • What other word can be used in place of _____	• One question I had as I read was: _____ • What am I thinking as I read? _____
Summarize	**Predict**
• What is the main event in this section? _____ • What does the author want me to remember? _____	• What will the next section be about? _____ • How does my own experience help me make predictions?

**Level C
Note-Taking Chart**

Extensive Practice

After reading, the Respond activities provide followup to the pretaught strategies and ensure ample skills practice.

Theme Book for Listening Comprehension and Main Idea Practice in The Basics

---

COMPREHENSION: RELATE MAIN IDEA AND DETAILS

Read and Think Together

Make two diagrams to tell about the main ideas of *Families*. Follow these steps.

1 Think about pages 4–19 in the book. What are the pages mainly about? Write a sentence in a box.

> Families do a lot of things together.

2 Think of details from the book that tell about this main idea. Add them to your diagram.

> Families do a lot of things together.
> They love and care for one another.

3 Make a new main idea diagram for pages 20–26 of the book.

> Children live in many kinds of families.
> Some have brothers and sisters, and some do not.

4 Use your main idea diagrams to tell a partner about *Families*.

from The Basics Bookshelf

FAMILIES

THEME BOOK
This photo essay shows how family members everywhere love and care for each other.

▼ **MAIN IDEA AND DETAILS**
The Basics

Reading Selection and Main Idea Practice in Level A

Respond to the Autobiography
Check Your Understanding

SUM IT UP

Relate Main Ideas and Details Study the tree diagram for pages 144–145 of "My Best Friend." Then make diagrams for Parts 2 and 3.

Tree Diagram for Part 1

Main Idea	Details
Lillie and Lessie were best friends	They liked to play together.
	They visited each other.
	They made frog houses together.
	They liked to talk and talk.

Write a Paragraph Use the tree diagram for Part 1 to write your paragraph. Follow these steps:

• Write a **topic sentence** to tell the main idea.
• Write details to support the main idea.
• Write a **concluding sentence** to sum up your paragraph.

> Lessie and Lillie were best friends. They liked to play together. They visited each other every chance they got. They made frog houses together. They liked to talk and talk. **They had fun being best friends.**

Now write paragraphs for Parts 2 and 3. Use your tree diagrams for ideas.

THINK IT OVER

Discuss Talk about these questions with a partner.

1. **Opinion** Would Lessie be a good friend? Why or why not?
2. **Author's Purpose** Why do you think Lessie wrote her autobiography?
3. **Comparisons** How would Lillie and Lessie's story be different if they grew up today? How would it be the same?
4. **Personal Experience** Do you have your life all planned out, like Lessie and Lillie did? Explain.

EXPRESS YOURSELF
▶ EXPRESS LIKES AND DISLIKES

Think about the qualities you like and dislike in a best friend. Share your ideas with the class. Then make a large class T-chart. Write the qualities that most people said.

▼ **MAIN IDEA AND DETAILS**
Level A

Practice

Level A

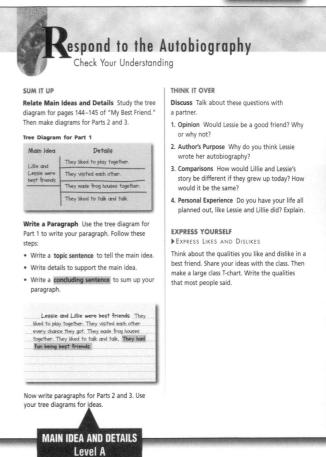

SUM IT UP

Relate Main Ideas and Details

DIRECTIONS Read the story. Add details from the story to finish the tree diagram.

> **Best Buddies**
> Felix and Rosario are best friends. They work together in math. After school, they play softball. Sometimes Rosario goes to Felix's house. They do their homework. Then they like to watch the basketball game on television.

Main Idea	Details
Felix and Rosario are best friends.	

DIRECTIONS Write a paragraph about Felix and Rosario. Use the ideas in your tree diagram.

Tell the main idea in your **topic sentence**. _____

Give **details** to tell more about the main idea. _____

Main Idea Practice in the Reading Practice Book

Reading Selection and Main Idea Practice in Level B

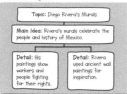

Respond to the Essay
Check Your Understanding

SUM IT UP

Relate Main Ideas and Details Make a main idea diagram for each section of the essay.

Main Idea Diagram

> Topic: Diego Rivera's Murals
>
> Main Idea: Rivera's murals celebrate the people and history of Mexico.
>
> Detail: His paintings show workers and people fighting for their rights.
>
> Detail: Rivera used ancient wall paintings for inspiration.

Write a Paragraph Use the main idea diagram to write a paragraph. A paragraph is a group of sentences that all tell about the same idea. One sentence gives the **main idea** of the paragraph. The other sentences give details that support the main idea.

Example:

Diego Rivera's Murals

Diego Rivera painted walls to celebrate Mexico's history. He painted people hard at work. He also painted people fighting for their rights. Rivera got some of his inspiration from ancient murals of Teotihuacán.

THINK IT OVER

Discuss and Write Talk about these questions with a partner. Write the answers.

1. **Cause and Effect** Why have people in the past and in the present created talking walls? Why are they important?

2. **Comparison** How do you think viewers feel about each of the talking walls in the essay? How are each of their messages similar?

3. **Conclusions** If you were a painter or architect, how would you represent the people of the U.S. in a mural? Why?

4. **Judgments** Imagine that you could leave a message on the fence of someone whom you admire. Whose fence would it be? Explain what tribute you would write and why.

EXPRESS YOURSELF EXPRESS OPINIONS

Tell a group about your favorite wall from the essay. Give three reasons that tell why you like that wall. Think about the way it looks, how it makes you feel, and the message it gives.

**▲ MAIN IDEA AND DETAILS
Level B**

Reading Selection and Main Idea Practice in Level C

Respond to the Photo Essay
Check Your Understanding

SUM IT UP

Relate Main Idea and Details Share your details for one section with your group. What is the main idea? Complete a chart to share with the class.

Main Idea and Details Chart

> Section Title: ___Curtain Up!___
>
> **Main Idea:** This section describes what it is like to watch the opening of The Lion King play.
>
> Detail: The performance starts in New York City a little after 8 o'clock.
>
> Detail: The Lion King is a stage musical about a young lion.
>
> Detail: Actors dressed in fantastic masks and costumes play the animals.

Write a Summary With your class, brainstorm several main idea statements for the entire selection. Take a vote for the best one. Then list details that support your main idea. Cross out the unimportant details.

Example:

Important detail: The Lion King is a stage musical about a young lion.

Unimportant detail: It starts a little after 8 o'clock.

Use the important details that remain on your list to write a summary of "The Lion King Goes to Broadway."

THINK IT OVER

Discuss and Write Talk about these questions with a partner. Write the answers.

1. **Analyze Information** Why did Julie Taymor feel it was important to show the actors' faces?

2. **Paraphrase** Tell a partner what a photo essay is like.

3. **Personal Experience** What creative ideas have you had? How have you accomplished them?

EXPRESS YOURSELF ▶DESCRIBE

Look at the photographs in the selection. Choose an animal costume and describe it to your partner. Include details about its size, how it is made, how it is worn, and how it moves. What makes this costume like the animal it represents?

**▲ MAIN IDEA AND DETAILS
Level C**

Level B

SUM IT UP

Relate Main Ideas and Details

DIRECTIONS Complete the main idea diagram for each topic from "Talking Walls." Then write two paragraphs on a separate sheet of paper. Tell about one topic in each paragraph.

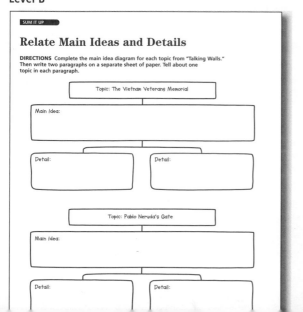

> Topic: The Vietnam Veterans Memorial
>
> Main Idea:
>
> Detail:
>
> Detail:
>
> Topic: Pablo Neruda's Gate
>
> Main Idea:
>
> Detail:
>
> Detail:

Level C

SUM IT UP

Relate Main Idea and Details

DIRECTIONS Read the article Rafael wrote for his school newspaper. Then complete the main idea and details chart.

> **A Great Stage Show!**
>
> *The Lion King* was much better as a stage play than as a movie. Seeing the live production was an experience I won't forget.
>
> When you see real actors dressed in elaborate costumes, it really captures your imagination. A movie just can't match that. Julie Taymor, who has worked on other Broadway productions, was the main designer. She and her team did a great job creating the amazing costumes.
>
> The sets and the lighting were also wonderful. I thought the atmosphere of Africa was better in the stage play than in the movie. There were some great special effects, too. For instance, when the lake dried up, I had to remind myself that it was a trick of the eye.
>
> Seeing the actors in person, instead of on a movie screen, was thrilling. Watching them on stage, I really thought they were jungle creatures. They trotted, slithered, and glided across the stage like real-life animals.
>
> The costumes, the sets, the lighting, and the performances made the stage play great. It was more exciting than any movie I have ever seen.

Main Idea and Details Chart

> Main Idea:
>
> Detail:
>
> Detail:
>
> Detail:

DIRECTIONS Write a summary of the article. Use information from the chart.

Language Development in *High Point*

Natural Language Models

Each theme begins with a song, poem, chant, story, or speech on tape. These interactive, motivational experiences spark language, model specific language functions or structures, and provide context for developing vocabulary and grammar skills.

The Basics

The Basics Student Book and Tape **SONG**

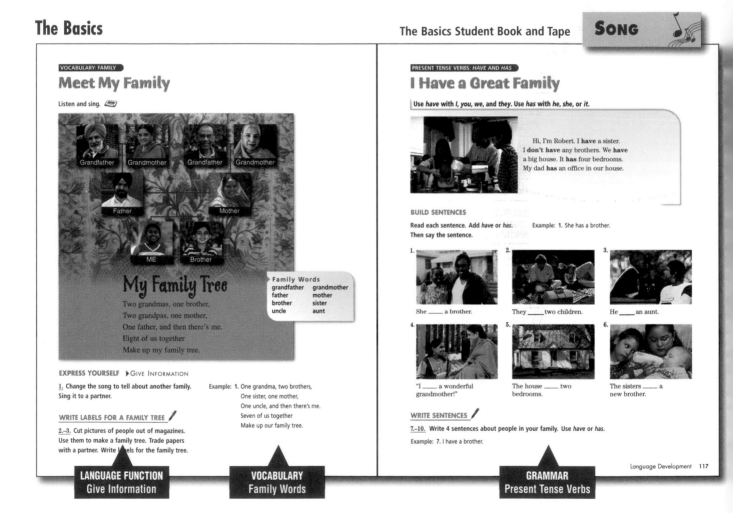

VOCABULARY: FAMILY

Meet My Family

Listen and sing.

Grandfather Grandmother Grandfather Grandmother

Father Mother

ME Brother

My Family Tree

Two grandmas, one brother,
Two grandpas, one mother,
One father, and then there's me.
Eight of us together
Make up my family tree.

Family Words

grandfather	grandmother
father	mother
brother	sister
uncle	aunt

EXPRESS YOURSELF ▶ GIVE INFORMATION

<u>1.</u> Change the song to tell about another family. Sing it to a partner.

WRITE LABELS FOR A FAMILY TREE ✎

<u>2.–3.</u> Cut pictures of people out of magazines. Use them to make a family tree. Trade papers with a partner. Write labels for the family tree.

Example: 1. One grandma, two brothers,
One sister, one mother,
One uncle, and then there's me.
Seven of us together
Make up our family tree.

PRESENT TENSE VERBS: *HAVE* AND *HAS*

I Have a Great Family

Use *have* with *I, you, we,* and *they.* Use *has* with *he, she,* or *it.*

Hi, I'm Robert. I **have** a sister. I **don't have** any brothers. We **have** a big house. It **has** four bedrooms. My dad **has** an office in our house.

BUILD SENTENCES

Read each sentence. Add *have* or *has.* Then say the sentence.

Example: 1. She has a brother.

1. She ____ a brother.

2. They ____ two children.

3. He ____ an aunt.

4. "I ____ a wonderful grandmother!"

5. The house ____ two bedrooms.

6. The sisters ____ a new brother.

WRITE SENTENCES ✎

<u>7.–10.</u> Write 4 sentences about people in your family. Use *have* or *has.*

Example: 7. I have a brother.

Language Development 117

LANGUAGE FUNCTION
Give Information

VOCABULARY
Family Words

GRAMMAR
Present Tense Verbs

Build Language and Vocabulary

DESCRIBE

Listen to this rap about the gods and goddesses of ancient Greece.

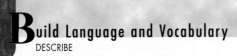

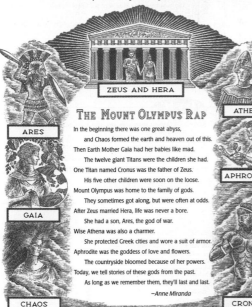

ZEUS AND HERA

ARES

ATHENA

APHRODITE

GAIA

THE MOUNT OLYMPUS RAP

In the beginning there was one great abyss,
    and Chaos formed the earth and heaven out of this.
Then Earth Mother Gaia had her babies like mad.
    The twelve giant Titans were the children she had.
One Titan named Cronus was the father of Zeus.
    His five other children were soon on the loose.
Mount Olympus was home to the family of gods.
    They sometimes got along, but were often at odds.
After Zeus married Hera, life was never a bore.
    She had a son, Ares, the god of war.
Wise Athena was also a charmer.
    She protected Greek cities and wore a suit of armor.
Aphrodite was the goddess of love and flowers.
    The countryside bloomed because of her powers.
Today, we tell stories of these gods from the past.
    As long as we remember them, they'll last and last.

–Anne Miranda

CHAOS

CRONUS

266 Unit 5 | Traditions

LANGUAGE FUNCTION
Describe

MAKE A CHARACTER CHART

Work with the group to list all the characters in the poem on a chart. Also record what each character did. Follow this model:

Name	What Character Did	
Chaos	formed earth and heaven	
Gaia	had the 12 Titans	

BUILD YOUR VOCABULARY

Describing Words Look at the pictures of the gods and goddesses on page 266. Think of a word to describe each one, or choose one from the **Word Bank**. Add a third column to your chart. In it, write a word to describe each character:

Name	What Character Did	What Character Was Like
Chaos	formed earth and heaven	powerful
Gaia	had the 12 Titans	strong

Word Bank
beautiful
big
dark
fierce
powerful
strong
tall
ugly

VOCABULARY
Describing
Words

USE LANGUAGE STRUCTURES ▶ COMPLETE SENTENCES

Writing: Describe Greek Gods Choose a Greek god or goddess. Use the information from the character chart to write two complete sentences. Tell what the god or goddess did, and what he or she was like. Be sure each sentence includes a subject and a predicate.

Example:
Athena protected Greek cities. She was powerful.

GRAMMAR
Complete
Sentences

Build Language and Vocabulary 267

Build Language and Vocabulary

TELL A STORY

Listen to this tale from Vietnam about a rooster who learns what matters most to him.

The Rooster and the Jewel

A VIETNAMESE TALE

MAKE A STORY MAP

Work with a group to plan a story about something that matters most to you. Choose the object or event. Then fill out a story map to name the characters, tell the setting, and outline the events in the plot.

Characters	Setting
Beginning	
Middle	
Ending	

BUILD YOUR VOCABULARY

Descriptive Words Think of words you will use to describe the story's characters and setting. Collect them in the charts.

Character	What is the character like?	What does the character do?	How, when, and where does the character do things?
Yolanda	young smart	She skates. She seems to fly.	quickly before dark through the park

Setting	What can you see?	What can you hear?	What can you smell?	What can you taste?	What can you touch?
an afternoon in a park	trees lake	birds traffic	smoke food cooking	hamburger	earth grass

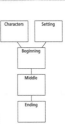 **VOCABULARY**
Describing Words
Story Elements

USE LANGUAGE STRUCTURES

▶ ADJECTIVES, ADVERBS, AND PREPOSITIONAL PHRASES

Speaking: Tell a Story Use your story map and the descriptive words in your charts to tell your story. Divide the story into parts so that each member of your group will have a part to tell.

Example:
Yolanda **quickly** gathered her skates and went **to the park**. She wanted to skate all **around the lake before dark**. She seemed to fly **through the park**, but then made a **sudden** stop. There **in the trees** she saw flames and smelled smoke. . . .

GRAMMAR
Adjectives
Adverbs
Prepositions

144 Unit 3 | Dreams and Decisions

LANGUAGE FUNCTION
Tell a Story

Build Language and Vocabulary 145

Systematic Grammar Instruction

The Instructional Overhead for Build Language and Vocabulary introduces the grammar skill. Followup lessons build skills in a logical sequence.

ADD DETAILS TO SENTENCES

You can add adjectives, adverbs, or prepositional phrases to a sentence to make it more interesting.

A squirrel scrambles.

A red squirrel scrambles quickly across the garden.
adjective — adverb — prepositional phrase

1. An **adjective** describes a noun or pronoun.

   The **huge** barn has a **blue** door. It is **full** of animals.

2. An **adverb** tells "how," "where," or "when." Adverbs usually tell more about a verb.

   We pet the bull **carefully**. The chickens live **outside**.

3. A prepositional phrase also tells "where" or "when." It starts with a **preposition** and ends with a noun or pronoun.

   The pigs live **across** the barnyard.
   prepositional phrase

Try It!

Add details to these sentences. Use adjectives, adverbs, and prepositional phrases.

1. The rooster ran home. | 3. The chicks found nothing to eat.
2. I lost the jewel. | 4. I saw the animals.

Instructional Overhead

Level B Student Book: Unit 3

B uild Language and Vocabulary
TELL A STORY

L isten to this tale from Vietnam about a rooster who learns what matters most to him.

The Rooster and the Jewel
A VIETNAMESE TALE

MAKE A STORY

Work with a grou...
to you. Choose th...
the characters, tel...

BUILD YOUR VO...

Descriptive Words Think of words you will use to describe the story's characters and setting. Collect them in the charts.

Character	What is the character like?	What does the character do?	How, when, and where does the character do things?
Yolanda	young smart	She skates. She seems to fly.	quickly before dark through the park

Setting	What can you see?	What can you hear?	What can you smell?	What can you taste?	What can you touch?
an afternoon in a park	trees lake	birds traffic	smoke food cooking	hamburger	earth grass

USE LANGUAGE STRUCTURES

▶ ADJECTIVES, ADVERBS, AND PREPOSITIONAL PHRASES

Speaking: Tell a Story Use your story map and the descriptive words in your charts to tell your story. Divide the story into parts so that each member of your group will have a part to tell.

Example:

Yolanda **quickly** gathered her skates and went **to the park**. She wanted to skate all **around the lake before dark**. She seemed to fly **through the park**, but then made a **sudden** stop. There **in the trees** she saw flames and smelled smoke. . . .

GRAMMAR INTRODUCTION
Adjectives
Adverbs
Prepositions

144 Unit 3 | Dreams and Decisions

Build Language and Vocabulary 145

Practice

*Abundant practice for each grammar skill in the **Language Practice Book** helps students master the complexities of English and transfer skills to writing.*

Grammar Practice in the Language Practice Book, Level B Unit 3

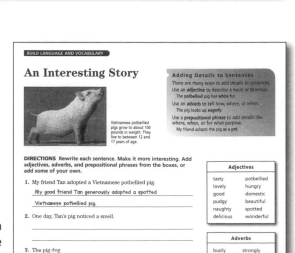

BUILD LANGUAGE AND VOCABULARY

An Interesting Story

Vietnamese potbellied pigs grow to about 100 pounds in weight. They live to between 12 and 17 years of age.

Adding Details to Sentences
There are many ways to add details to sentences.
Use an **adjective** to describe a noun or pronoun.
The potbellied pig has **white** fur.
Use an **adverb** to tell how, where, or when.
The pig looks up **eagerly**.
Use a **prepositional phrase** to add details like where, when, or for what purpose.
My friend adopts the pig **as a pet**.

DIRECTIONS Rewrite each sentence. Make it more interesting. Add adjectives, adverbs, and prepositional phrases from the boxes, or add some of your own.

1. My friend Tan adopted a Vietnamese potbellied pig.

   My good friend Tan generously adopted a spotted

   Vietnamese potbellied pig.

2. One day, Tan's pig noticed a smell.

3. The pig dug

4. The sofa was destroyed.

5. Tan says, "I recommend you learn about pigs."

Adjectives	
tasty	potbellied
lovely	hungry
good	domestic
pudgy	beautiful
naughty	spotted
delicious	wonderful

Adverbs	
busily	strongly
quickly	generously
inside	almost
nearly	always

Prepositional Phrases
with his nose
for a treat
before adopting one
within seconds
under the sofa

Level B Student Book: Unit 3

Respond to the Story, continued
Language Arts and Literature

▶ **GRAMMAR IN CONTEXT**

USE ADJECTIVES

Learn About Adjectives An adjective is a word that describes, or tells about, a noun.

Adjectives can tell how many or how much.

> Yenna waited **four** years.
> Yenna had **little** interest in marrying.

Adjectives can tell which one.

> Yenna shook out the **first** shirt.

Adjectives can tell what something is like.

> The ginger was **fragrant** and **moist**.
> The **young** man asked Yenna to marry him.

Proper adjectives come from proper nouns. They begin with a capital letter.

> Chang was from China. He was **Chinese**.

Add Adjectives Expand these sentences with adjectives.

1. Yenna sewed with _____ needles and _____ thread.

2. The _____ man held the _____ ginger in his _____ hand.

Practice Write this paragraph. Add an adjective in each blank.

> The _____ streets of Chinatown are interesting to see. There are _____ buildings. Some have _____ walls and _____ windows. One building has a _____ tower with _____ roof.

▶ **WRITING/SPEAKING**

WRITE AN OUTCOME

Think of the new endings to the story you discussed with your group in the Sum It Up activity on page 155. How would the characters' actions change in order to cause a new outcome? Would their goals also change? Make a chart to organize your ideas. Then write the new outcome.

❶ **Complete a Chart** Fill in a new Goal-and-Outcome Chart like the one you made on page 155.

❷ **Write a Draft** Write the main events of the beginning, middle, and end of the new story. Include dialogue that shows what the characters' goals are.

❸ **Edit Your Work** Add, change, or take out text to make your story more interesting. Do the characters have believable goals? What is the final outcome? Finally, check for correct spelling, punctuation, and grammar.

❹ **Read and Discuss** Read your work in a group. Discuss the goals and actions that caused the new outcomes.

> For more about the **writing process,** see Handbook pages 408–413.

GRAMMAR REVIEW
Adjectives

Level B Student Book: Unit 3

Respond to the Article, continued
Language Arts and Literature

▶ **GRAMMAR IN CONTEXT**

USE ADJECTIVES THAT COMPARE

Learn About Comparative Adjectives A **comparative adjective** compares two things. To make the comparison, add **–er** to the adjective and use the word **than**.

> Neshy's hair is **longer than** Suzy's.

If the adjective is a long word, use **more** or **less**.

> Neshy is **more independent than** Suzy.

Learn About Superlative Adjectives A **superlative adjective** compares three or more things. Add **–est** to the adjective. Use **the** before the adjective.

> Suzy is **the fastest** runner in her class.

If the adjective is long, use **the most** or **the least**.

> **The most important** thing to the twins is staying in touch.

Practice Write these sentences. Use the correct form of the adjective in parentheses.

1. Some hearing-impaired people have a (great) hearing loss than others do.

2. Gallaudet is perhaps the (fine) school in the world for hearing-impaired students.

3. When they learned sign language, the twins were (confident) than before.

4. The (difficult) time of all came after the twins were separated.

▶ **TECHNOLOGY/MEDIA**

▶ **WRITING**

WRITE TO A TWIN

With a partner, take the roles of Suzy and Neshy. Pretend that you have been apart for one month. Write a series of letters or e-mails to each other.

❶ **Choose a Topic** Here are some possible topics for your first letters:
- future dreams or plans
- life in your new city or home
- an upcoming visit
- family and friends

❷ **Start the Series** One partner writes the first letter or e-mail. The other partner reads it and writes back. Write several more letters or e-mails back and forth.

❸ **Check Your Work** Check your work before sending it to your "twin." Check for correct spelling and punctuation.

> For more about **e-mail,** see Handbook page 382.

SEQUENTIAL GRAMMAR SKILL
Comparative Adjectives

GRAMMAR: ADJECTIVES

Historic Letters

DIRECTIONS Work with a small group. Read the article. Circle the adjectives. Write each adjective in the correct column of the chart.

In 1850, a boat sailed into the (crowded) harbor in San Francisco. On the boat were Louise Clappe, her husband, and her two sisters. They had come all the way from (central) Massachusetts. Leaving his wife in San Francisco, Dr. Fayette Clappe traveled to a rough camp in the Sierras to open a medical practice. Eventually, Louise joined him.

Over fifteen months, Louise wrote twenty-three letters from the camps. Her first letter describes her wild journey to the camp. The letters describe a distant time in American history. They tell about the French and Spanish miners and people from around the world. They describe the steep mountains, the brilliant river, and the crude buildings.

Louise wrote her last letter in November, 1852. After that, she returned to San Francisco and taught school for twenty-four years. She died in New Jersey in 1906.

> **Adjectives**
> An adjective describes a noun or pronoun. Adjectives can tell how many, how much, which one, or what something is like.
> The second letter describes the important rooms in the grand Empire Hotel.
> A **proper adjective** comes from a proper noun.
> The letters bring American history to life.

How Many/ How Much	Which One	What Something Is Like	Proper Adjectives
1. _____	5. central	9. crowded	16. _____
2. _____	6. _____	10. _____	17. _____
3. _____	7. _____	11. _____	18. _____
4. _____	8. _____	12. _____	
		13. _____	
		14. _____	
		15. _____	

MORE ABOUT ADJECTIVES Work with your group to add sparkle to the passage.

GRAMMAR: ADJECTIVES THAT COMPARE

Family Comparisons

Whitewater rafting is a thrilling adventure for many.

> **Adjectives That Compare**
> A **comparative adjective** compares two things.
> My sister is quieter than I am.
> She is less sociable than me, too.
> A **superlative adjective** compares three or more things.
> I am the **friendliest** person in the family.
> I am the **most sociable** person in my home!
> Use **–er** and **–est** for most two-syllable adjectives. Use less / more and least / most for words with three or more syllables.

DIRECTIONS Complete each sentence. Write the correct form of the adjective in parentheses.

1. Jayesh is __more adventurous__ than his twin brother, Kuval. (**adventurous**)

2. He wants to raft down the _____ river in the West. (**wild**)

3. He wants to climb the _____ peak on the continent. (**high**)

4. Jayesh is _____ than Kuval. (**studious**)

5. Kuval is _____ than his brother. (**calm**)

6. To Kuval, drawing is the _____ thing in the world! (**exciting**)

DIRECTIONS Write sentences to compare people you know. Use the correct forms of the adjectives in the box or some of your own.

7. __My sister is less confident than I am.__

8. _____

9. _____

10. _____

creative
independent
tidy
nice
confident
funny
strong
athletic

More Practice on Adjectives in the Language Practice Book, Level B Unit 3

35

Writing Instruction in *High Point*

Fundamentals of Writing

The Basics level addresses the fundamentals of writing—from sentences to an expository paragraph.

The Basics Student Book

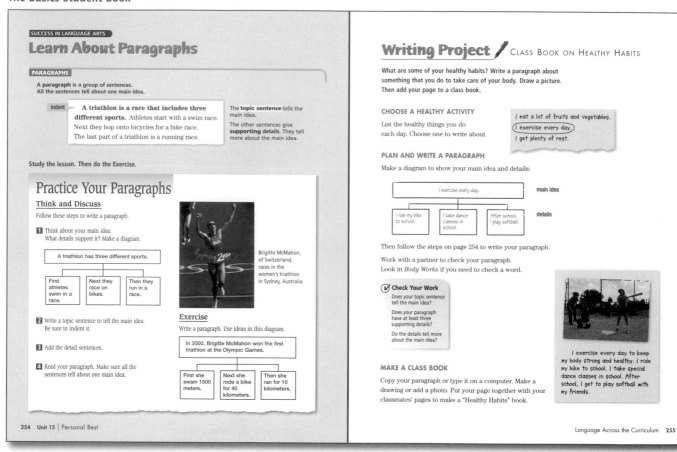

SUCCESS IN LANGUAGE ARTS
Learn About Paragraphs

PARAGRAPHS

A **paragraph** is a group of sentences. All the sentences tell about one main idea.

indent   **A triathlon is a race that includes three different sports.** Athletes start with a swim race. Next they hop onto bicycles for a bike race. The last part of a triathlon is a running race.

The **topic sentence** tells the main idea.

The other sentences give **supporting details**. They tell more about the main idea.

Study the lesson. Then do the Exercise.

Practice Your Paragraphs

Think and Discuss

Follow these steps to write a paragraph.

1 Think about your main idea. What details support it? Make a diagram.

| A triathlon has three different sports. |
| First athletes swim in a race. | Next they race on bikes. | Then they run in a race. |

2 Write a topic sentence to tell the main idea. Be sure to indent it.

3 Add the detail sentences.

4 Read your paragraph. Make sure all the sentences tell about one main idea.

Brigitte McMahon, of Switzerland, races in the women's triathlon in Sydney, Australia.

Exercise

Write a paragraph. Use ideas in this diagram.

| In 2000, Brigitte McMahon won the first triathlon at the Olympic Games. |
| First she swam 1500 meters. | Next she rode a bike for 40 kilometers. | Then she ran for 10 kilometers. |

254   Unit 15 | Personal Best

Writing Project ✏ CLASS BOOK ON HEALTHY HABITS

What are some of your healthy habits? Write a paragraph about something that you do to take care of your body. Then add your page to a class book.

CHOOSE A HEALTHY ACTIVITY

List the healthy things you do each day. Choose one to write about.

I eat a lot of fruits and vegetables.
(I exercise every day.)
I get plenty of rest.

PLAN AND WRITE A PARAGRAPH

Make a diagram to show your main idea and details:

| I exercise every day. | **main idea** |
| I ride my bike to school. | I take dance classes in school. | After school, I play softball. | **details** |

Then follow the steps on page 254 to write your paragraph.

Work with a partner to check your paragraph. Look in *Body Works* if you need to check a word.

✓ Check Your Work

Does your topic sentence tell the main idea?

Does your paragraph have at least three supporting details?

Do the details tell more about the main idea?

MAKE A CLASS BOOK

Copy your paragraph or type it on a computer. Make a drawing or add a photo. Put your page together with your classmates' pages to make a "Healthy Habits" book.

I exercise every day to keep my body strong and healthy. I ride my bike to school. I take special dance classes in school. After school, I get to play softball with my friends.

Language Across the Curriculum   255

Writing Support

Writing instruction is scaffolded to ensure success.

Drafting Support

The Basics

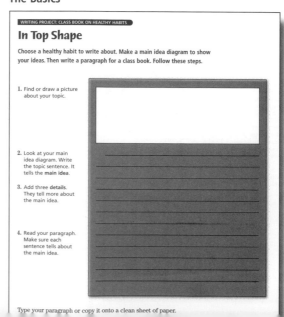

WRITING PROJECT: CLASS BOOK ON HEALTHY HABITS
In Top Shape

Choose a healthy habit to write about. Make a main idea diagram to show your ideas. Then write a paragraph for a class book. Follow these steps.

1. Find or draw a picture about your topic.

2. Look at your main idea diagram. Write the topic sentence. It tells the **main idea**.

3. Add three **details**. They tell more about the main idea.

4. Read your paragraph. Make sure each sentence tells about the main idea.

Type your paragraph or copy it onto a clean sheet of paper.

Writing Strategies and Applications

Writing Projects in each unit give experience with the modes and forms of writing represented in the standards and assessed on standardized tests.

HE WRITING PROCESS AT LEVELS A–C

Students first study the writing mode through professional and student models and explore ways to organize their writing.

Level B Student Book: Unit 3 Writing Project

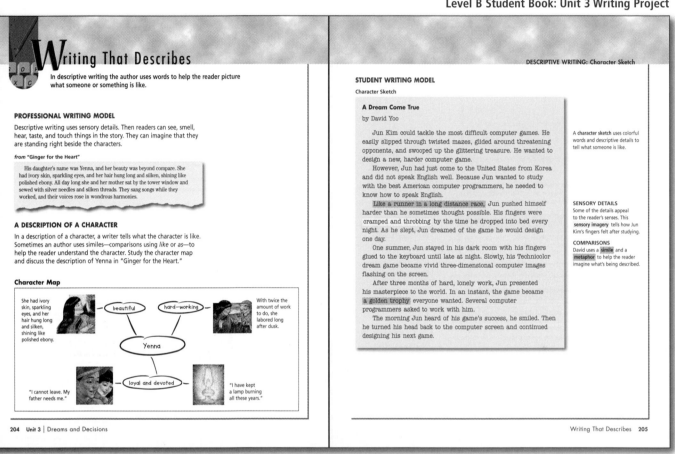

Support for Studying Writing Models

Writing Strategies and Applications, continued

THE WRITING PROCESS AT LEVELS A–C

- Next, students are guided step-by-step through the entire writing process with visual support.

- The Reflect and Evaluate features challenge students to self-assess so they can continually improve their writing.

- The Writer's Craft teaches such skills as word choice and elaboration to help students shape their writing. Language models illustrate quality differences.

Level B Student Book: Unit 3 Writing Project

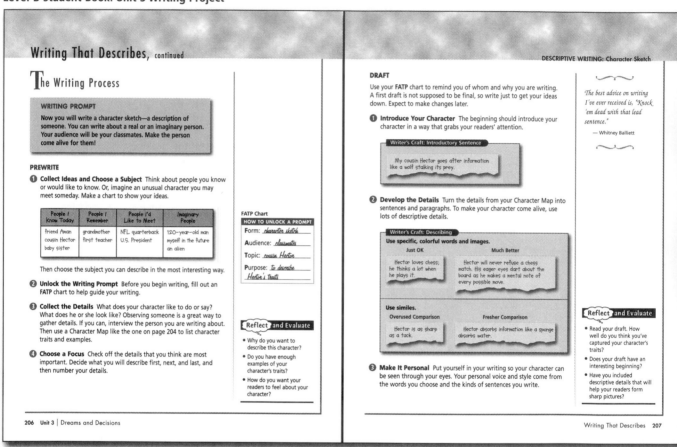

Level B

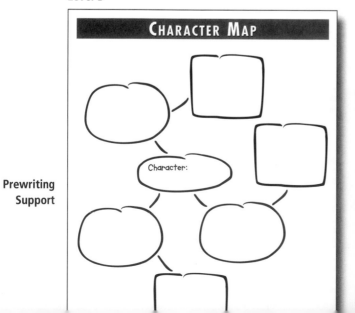

Prewriting Support

Level B

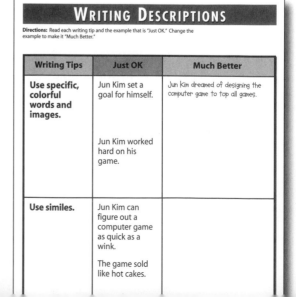

Writer's Craft Support

THE WRITING PROCESS AT LEVELS A–C

- Revising strategies model language for effective participation in peer conferences.

- Technology features help students learn to write and revise their work on the computer.

- Grammar in context relates the unit's grammar focus to the writing.

Level B Student Book: Unit 3 Writing Project

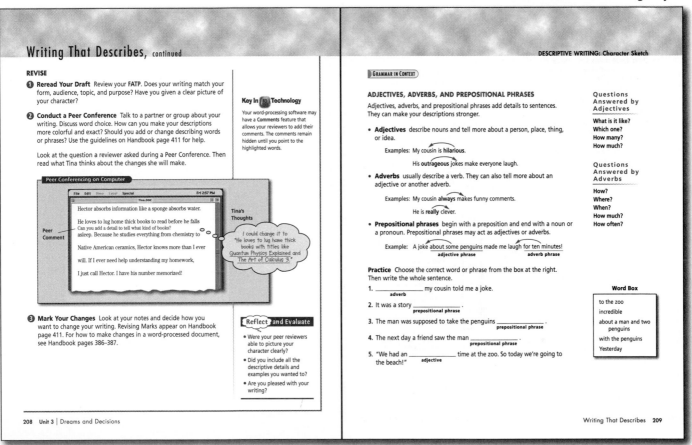

Level B

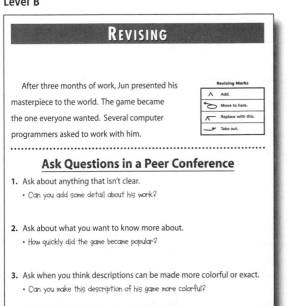

Revising Support

Writing Strategies and Applications, continued

THE WRITING PROCESS IN LEVELS A–C

- Editing and proofreading strategies help students achieve accuracy in written conventions.

- Technology features help students edit and publish work on the computer.

Level B Student Book: Unit 3 Writing Project

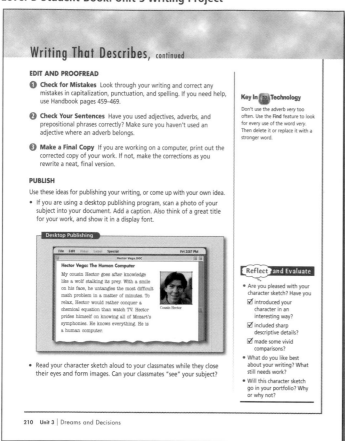

Practice in Written Conventions

Editing and Proofreading Support

Level B

EDITING AND PROOFREADING

Directions: Read each sentence. Check for errors in capitalization, spelling, and punctuation. Use the Proofreading Marks to correct the mistakes

1. However, Jun had just come to the United states from Korea and did not speak English well?

2. One summer, jun stayed in his dark room with his fingers glud to the keyboard until late at night.

3. The Morning Jun heard of his game's success, he smiled.

Proofreading Marks

∧	Add.
⩓	Add a comma.
⊙	Add a period.
≡	Capitalize.
/	Make lowercase.
⌐	Take out.
¶	Indent.

Directions: Read the paragraph. Check for errors in capitalization, spelling, and punctuation. Check whether adjectives and adverbs are used correctly. Use the Proofreading Marks to correct the mistakes.

Like a runner in a long distance race, Jun pushed himself hard than he sometimes thot possible. His fingers were cramped and throbbing by the time he dropped into bed all night as he slept, Jun dreamed of the game he would design one day.

Written Conventions

Handbooks at each level support students in applying the written conventions of English.

Grammar Support in Handbook

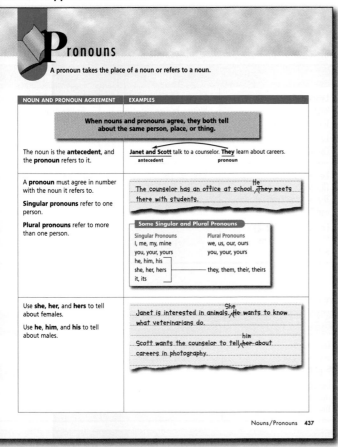

Pronouns

A pronoun takes the place of a noun or refers to a noun.

NOUN AND PRONOUN AGREEMENT	EXAMPLES
When nouns and pronouns agree, they both tell about the same person, place, or thing.	
The noun is the **antecedent**, and the **pronoun** refers to it.	Janet and Scott talk to a counselor. They learn about careers. antecedent pronoun
A **pronoun** must agree in number with the noun it refers to. **Singular pronouns** refer to one person. **Plural pronouns** refer to more than one person.	The counselor has an office at school. They meets there with students. (He) **Some Singular and Plural Pronouns** Singular Pronouns: I, me, my, mine; you, your, yours; he, him, his; she, her, hers; it, its Plural Pronouns: we, us, our, ours; you, your, yours; they, them, their, theirs
Use **she, her,** and **hers** to tell about females. Use **he, him,** and **his** to tell about males.	Janet is interested in animals. He wants to know what veterinarians do. (She) Scott wants the counselor to tell her about careers in photography. (him)

Nouns/Pronouns **437**

Punctuation Support in Handbook

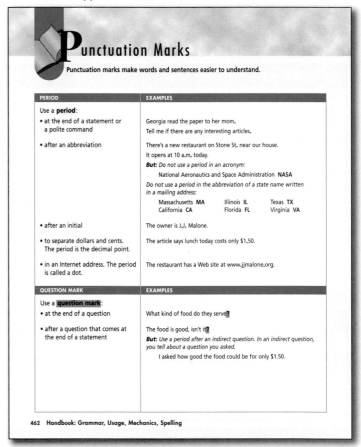

Punctuation Marks

Punctuation marks make words and sentences easier to understand.

PERIOD	EXAMPLES
Use a **period**:	
• at the end of a statement or a polite command	Georgia read the paper to her mom. Tell me if there are any interesting articles.
• after an abbreviation	There's a new restaurant on Stone St. near our house. It opens at 10 a.m. today. ***But:*** Do not use a period in an acronym: National Aeronautics and Space Administration NASA *Do not use a period in the abbreviation of a state name written in a mailing address:* Massachusetts **MA** Illinois **IL** Texas **TX** California **CA** Florida **FL** Virginia **VA**
• after an initial	The owner is J.J. Malone.
• to separate dollars and cents. The period is the decimal point.	The article says lunch today costs only $1.50.
• in an Internet address. The period is called a dot.	The restaurant has a Web site at www.jjmalone.org.

QUESTION MARK	EXAMPLES
Use a **question mark**:	
• at the end of a question	What kind of food do they serve?
• after a question that comes at the end of a statement	The food is good, isn't it? ***But:*** Use a period after an indirect question. In an indirect question, you tell about a question you asked. I asked how good the food could be for only $1.50.

462 Handbook: Grammar, Usage, Mechanics, Spelling

Level A

They Are a Team

DIRECTIONS Read the sentences. Write the correct pronouns.

1. **My friend and I** see a team of oxen. ___We___ watch the oxen work.
2. **The oxen** work together. _____ pull the plow.
3. **Mr. Davidov** guides the plow. _____ steers it.
4. **The plow** loosens the soil. _____ digs into the hard earth.
5. **The field** is bare now. ___It___ is ready for seeds.
6. **Sofia and Eva** are a team. _____ plant the seeds.
7. **Sofia** has some seeds. _____ drops the seeds into the ground.
8. Sofia tells **Eva,** "Take a rest. _____ are tired."

Subject Pronouns

A pronoun takes the place of a noun. A subject pronoun tells who does something.
The oxen pull the plow.
They pull the plow.

Subject Pronouns

One	More Than One
I	we
you	you
he, she, it	they

DIRECTIONS Write sentences about the picture. Use subject pronouns.

He steers the plow.
_____
_____
_____
_____

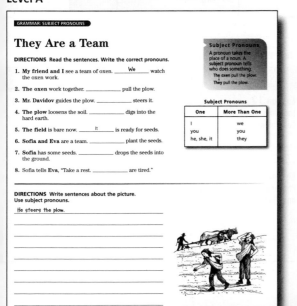

Level A

Thanks! You Helped Us!

Subject and Object Pronouns

A pronoun takes the place of a noun.
A subject pronoun tells who or what does something.
The man is in trouble.
He needs help.
An object pronoun follows a verb or a preposition.
Camila helps the man.
Camila rescues him.

Subject Pronouns

One	More Than One
I	we
you	you
he, she, it	they

Object Pronouns

One	More Than One
me	us
you	you
him, her, it	them

1. Camila is a rescue worker. She gets a call for help. ___subject___
2. A hiker is hurt. He needs help. _____
3. Camila's team goes to him. _____
4. They lower Camila down on a rope. _____
5. The team pulls them both up. _____

DIRECTIONS Read the thank-you note. Circle the correct pronouns.

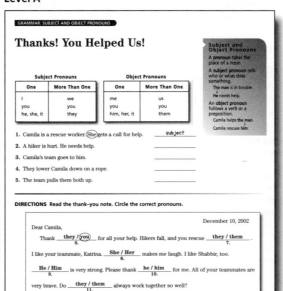

December 10, 2002

Dear Camila,

Thank ___they / you___ for all your help. Hikers fall, and you rescue ___they / them___
   6.   7.

I like your teammate, Katrina. ___She / Her___ makes me laugh. I like Shabbir, too.
                                8.

___He / Him___ is very strong. Please thank ___he / him___ for me. All of your teammates are
   9.   10.

very brave. Do ___they / them___ always work together so well?
                 11.

My family is very grateful. ___We / Us___ are all thankful for your help. My sister wants to
                              12.

Extensive Pronoun Practice in the Practice Books

Pacing Options

High Point is a flexible program whose pacing can be adjusted to one-hour, two-hour, or three-hour sessions.

The Basics

This level of **High Point** contains 18 units and an optional unit called Lakeside School. See page T10e of The Basics Teacher's Edition for the recommended pacing of Lakeside School.

3-HOUR INTERVENTION PACING
In this model, each unit takes one week. (Number of lessons in a unit varies from 13 to 16.)

UNIT 11	Day 1	Day 2	Day 3	Day 4	Day 5
Language Development (1 hour)	**Lesson 1** Introduce the Unit **Lesson 2** Vocabulary or Grammar Lesson	**Lessons 3–4** Vocabulary or Grammar Lessons	**Lesson 5** Vocabulary or Grammar Lesson **Lesson 12** Content Area Connection	**Lesson 13** Writing Project	**Lesson 13 (cont.)** Writing Project
Language and Literacy (2 hours)	**Lesson 6** The Basics Bookshelf: Theme Book Read-Alouds	**Lesson 8** High Frequency Words **Lesson 9 (Part 1)** Phonemic Awareness and Phonics	**Lesson 7** The Basics Bookshelf: Theme Book Comprehension and Retelling **Lesson 9 (Part 2)** Phonemic Awareness and Phonics	**Lesson 10** Reading and Spelling with Practice in Decodable Text	**Lesson 11** Independent Reading (decodable text), Comprehension, and Reading Fluency

DAILY PERIOD PACING
In this model, each unit takes about two weeks to complete.

UNIT 11 (Week 1)	Day 1	Day 2	Day 3	Day 4	Day 5
Language Development and Literacy (1 hour)	**Lesson 1** Introduce the Unit **Lesson 2** Vocabulary or Grammar Lesson	**Lessons 3–4** Vocabulary or Grammar Lessons	**Lesson 5** Vocabulary or Grammar Lesson **Lesson 6** The Basics Bookshelf: Theme Book Read-Alouds	**Lesson 7** The Basics Bookshelf: Theme Book Comprehension and Retelling	**Lesson 8** High Frequency Words **Lesson 9 (Part 1)** Phonemic Awareness and Phonics

UNIT 11 (Week 2)	Day 6	Day 7	Day 8	Day 9	Day 10
Language Development and Literacy (1 hour)	**Lesson 9 (Part 2)** Phonemic Awareness and Phonics	**Lesson 10** Reading and Spelling with Practice in Decodable Text	**Lesson 11** Independent Reading (decodable text), Comprehension, and Reading Fluency	**Lesson 12** Content Area Connection **Lesson 13** Writing Project	**Lesson 13 (cont.)** Writing Project

BLOCK SCHEDULE PACING
In this model, two or three sessions occur each week, so each unit takes about two weeks.

UNIT 11	Session 1	Session 2	Session 3	Session 4	Session 5	Session 6
Language Development (1 hour)	**Lesson 1** Introduce the Unit **Lesson 2** Vocabulary or Grammar Lesson	**Lessons 3–4** Vocabulary or Grammar Lessons	**Lesson 5** Vocabulary or Grammar Lesson	**Lesson 12** Language Across the Curriculum	**Lesson 13** Writing Project	**Lesson 13 (cont.)** Writing Project
Language and Literacy (1 to 1 1/2 hours)	**Lesson 6** The Basics Bookshelf: Theme Book Road-Alouds	**Lesson 7** The Basics Bookshelf: Theme Book Comprehension and Retelling **Lesson 8** High Frequency Words	**Lesson 9 (Part 1)** Phonemic Awareness and Phonics	**Lesson 9 (Part 2)** Phonemic Awareness and Phonics	**Lesson 10** Reading and Spelling with Practice in Decodable Text	**Lesson 11** Independent Reading (decodable text), Comprehension, and Reading Fluency

Levels A–C

Levels A–C of *High Point* each contain 5 units. Each unit contains 2 themes.

3-HOUR INTERVENTION PACING
In this model, each unit takes approximately 3 weeks. (Number of lessons per theme varies.)

LEVEL A, UNIT 1	Day 1	Day 2	Day 3	Day 4	Day 5
THEME 1	**THEME 1** **Lesson 1** • Introduce the Theme **Lesson 2** • Build Language and Vocabulary	**Lesson 3** Prepare to Read • Vocabulary • Reading Strategy **Lessons 4–5** Read the Selection	**Lesson 6** Respond to the Selection • Check Your Understanding activities **Lesson 7** Respond to the Selection • Language Arts and Literature activities	**Lesson 8** Respond to the Selection • Content Area Connections **Conduct Grammar Minilesson**	**Lesson 9** Build Language and Vocabulary **Lesson 10** Prepare to Read • Vocabulary • Reading Strategy

LEVEL A, UNIT 1	Day 6	Day 7	Day 8	Day 9	Day 10
THEME 1 and THEME 2	**Lessons 11–12** Read the Selection **Lesson 13** Respond to the Selection • Check Your Understanding activities	**Lesson 14** Respond to the Selection • Language Arts and Literature activities **Conduct Grammar Minilesson**	**Lesson 15** Respond to the Selection • Content Area Connections **Conduct Research Skills Minilesson**	**THEME 2** **Lesson 1** • Introduce the Theme **Lesson 2** Build Language and Vocabulary **Lesson 3** Prepare to Read • Vocabulary • Reading Strategy	**Lessons 4–5** Read the Selection **Lesson 6** Respond to the Selection • Check Your Understanding activities **Conduct Grammar Minilesson**

LEVEL A, UNIT 1	Day 11	Day 12	Day 13	Day 14	Day 15
THEME 2	**Lesson 7** Respond to the Selection • Language Arts and Content Area Connections **Conduct Grammar Minilesson**	**Lesson 8** Build Language and Vocabulary **Lesson 9** Prepare to Read • Vocabulary • Reading Strategy **Lessons 10–11** Read the Selection	**Lesson 12** Respond to the Selection • Check Your Understanding activities **Lesson 13** Respond to the Selection • Language Arts and Literature	**Lesson 14** Respond to the Selection • Content Area Connections **Conduct Grammar Minilesson**	**Lesson 15** Prepare to Read • Vocabulary • Reading Strategy **Lesson 16** Read and Respond to the Poem **Unit Debrief and Assessment**
Writing Project		Study Writing Models Write Together	Prewrite Draft	Revise Grammar in Context	Edit and Proofread Publish

The intervention program will last two years for the student who places at the beginning of The Basics.

DAILY PERIOD PACING

In this model, each unit takes 6-7 weeks to complete. The Activity Planners at the start of each unit in the Levels A–C Teacher's Editions show how to divide the units into daily periods. In general, each lesson takes about a day and the Writing Project is spread across the last week of each unit.

BLOCK SCHEDULE OR 2-HOUR SESSION PACING

In this model, two or three block schedule sessions occur each week such that each unit takes 6-7 weeks to complete. The Activity Planners at the start of each unit in the Levels A–C Teacher's Editions show how to divide the units into block schedule sessions. In general, two lessons can be completed per session and the Writing Project is spread across the last two weeks of the unit.

YEAR 1 33–36 weeks	The Basics	18-21 weeks
	Level A	15 weeks
YEAR 2 30 weeks	Level B	15 weeks
	Level C	15 weeks

Practice Book Contents and Homework Opportunities

- **Homework Opportunity**